To Mark,

Thank you for visiting Scranton.

Until we see each other again, you will be in my prayers.

your friend,

Deb

Designing Problem-Driven Instruction with Online Social Media

Designing Problem-Driven Instruction with Online Social Media

Edited by

Kay Kyeong-Ju Seo, Debra A. Pellegrino, and Chalee Engelhard

INFORMATION AGE PUBLISHING, INC.
Charlotte, NC • www.infoagepub.com

Library of Congress Cataloging-in-Publication Data

Designing problem-driven instruction with online social media / edited by Kay Kyeong-Ju Seo, Debra A. Pellegrino, and Chalee Engelhard.
p. cm.
Includes bibliographical references.
ISBN 978-1-61735-644-5 (pbk.) – ISBN 978-1-61735-645-2 (hardcover) – ISBN 978-1-61735-646-9 (ebook)
1. Internet in education. 2. Social media. I. Seo, Kay Kyeong-Ju. II. Pellegrino, Debra A. III. Engelhard, Chalee.
LB1044.87.D492 2011
371.33'44678–dc23
2011038822

CONTENTS

UNIT 3

HIGHER EDUCATION

UNIT 4

BEYOND THE CLASSROOM

PREFACE

Not too long ago, it was perfectly acceptable for instructors to be the fountain of knowledge and for students to come to the font to learn. However, more recently, the learning paradigm has shifted to reflect empowerment of the student and the instructor as a facilitator where they both go to the font, the instructor guides, and the student drives the learning experience. The unseen component added to this reallocation of roles is how the new generation of learners uses technology as a part of their everyday lives. They consistently use online social media tools, such as Twitter and Facebook, to email and text as a way to interact with their environment. Struggles exist as to understanding the ramifications of online social media and the implications it holds on the questionable success instructors may have while attempting to reach out to this new generation of students. How can an instructor meet the next generation of learners on a level that engages the student yet enhances learning at the same time?

This book serves to provide a vehicle for practitioners at all levels to expedite and successfully implement problem-driven instruction using online social media as an interface for enhanced learning experiences. For the novice user, the book enables confidence in utilizing this venue for instructional use. For experienced social media users, it provides evidence-based instruction and a decision-making framework and helps problem solve common issues that arise. Also, considering the levels at which instructors deliver their lessons, teachers in K–12 education, professors in higher education, and pre-service teacher candidates need to have instructional strategies available to them in order to facilitate online social media with problem-based learning. This publication seeks to elicit an understanding of how online social media and problem-driven instruction enhances student learning outcomes and to provide recommendations to teachers at all levels. Users will experience high satisfaction with implementing the techniques shared in this book, as their students will become more engaged in learning and have successful learning results.

The approach to the organization of this book is to create curiosity and interest of the reader from the beginning and to provide authentic examples of practical application throughout each of its four units. The venue of the book progressively moves from a smaller-scale, K–12 environment to a larger, global context. The first unit discusses underlying principles of problem-driven instruction and the current trends of online social media. It determines how an instructor can become obsolete in practice and outlines a path to change their classroom instruction to innovative pedagogy. The second unit takes a concentrated look at K–12 application. It offers insight into the collaborative use of online social media to support learning objectives in history, reading, and writing. Both chapters within this unit provide authentic examples of how online social media have the ability to enhance classroom practice in the K–12 environment. The third unit takes a step into higher education where the chapters focus on the use of wikis in collaborative learning, voice reflection in problem-based scenarios, and clinical reasoning using online social media. In particular, presentation of detailed cases to identify key design considerations and noting the interrelationship of learning objectives, problem choices, pedagogical practices, and implications for designing wiki-supported problem-driven instruction occur. Additionally, this unit demonstrates how blogging with voice-recorded reflections enables a platform for problem-driven instruction to meet definitive class-related objectives, whereas the use of YouTube videos produces the opportunity for interaction and feedback on increasing occupational therapy students' clinical reasoning skills. The final unit takes the reader out of the traditional classroom and into the community and the global setting. This unit provides a clear course for incorporation of online social media to increase the effectiveness of civic action-related youth, community service learning projects as well as design principles for problem-driven instruction with online social media based for networked learning particularly in Korean contexts.

Therefore, the organization and content of *Designing Problem-Driven Instruction with Online Social Media* takes the reader on a journey that invokes, a deeper understanding of the use of problem-driven instruction with online social media tools. A detailed path of how to implement these new tools becomes evident through each chapter. Lastly, readers will find that they will use this book as a reference tool when looking to augment online social media into everyday classroom practice regardless of the current educational setting in which they work.

UNIT 1

OVERVIEW

CHAPTER 1

GOING FROM OBSOLETE TO INNOVATIVE

Empowering Problem-Based Learning with Online Social Media

Chalee Engelhard and Kay Kyeong-Ju Seo

Becoming obsolete is more of a matter of stagnation than a willful act of making a choice to move in a purposeful direction. With current technological advances occurring almost daily, an instructor's ability to reach his or her students has the potential to diminish over time. This chapter embraces this concept and outlines a path to move from idleness to action. A case that is woven throughout the chapter represents a common occurrence in education after a course comes to an end—the moment of reflection that yields insights to what needs improvement the next time the course is delivered and decisions are made about what to do about it. The case provides a vehicle for how online social media (OSM) can enhance the ability of problem-based learning (PBL) to meet students on their terms and bring learning to a new level. The chapter shares examples of types of OSM tools that afford a foundation for education, including wikis, blogs, social bookmarking, virtual worlds, and multimedia. An in-depth look at specific avenues for implementation into the classroom consists of Facebook, wikis, Flickr, VoiceThread, Skype, and Second Life®. Taking the opportunity to venture outside a comfort zone

Designing Problem-Driven Instruction with Online Social Media, pages 3–20
Copyright © 2012 by Information Age Publishing

3

and move away from becoming obsolete involves changing a mindset and embracing the challenge of learning new modes of course delivery. Nevertheless, being willing to go on this venture will create a new ability to meet the students at the edge and take the leap of faith into a more contemporary course content design.{\abs}

INTRODUCTION

Becoming obsolete. This is not a phrase most people desire to be used in reference to themselves or their jobs. Yet we live in a world where keeping up with the latest technological advances is at the minimum time consuming and can be most intimidating. What is facilitating this change and driving the demand for technology to continue to develop into new and confounding configurations? The answer centers on student education where it is one of the most powerful driving forces behind this movement. Learners influence the preferred learning venues of today, and now it is in the format of online experiences. What vehicles are the preferred modes of delivery of information in order to keep the attention of today's students? How can we create engagement in an ever-changing world of technology and efficiency? In this chapter, we will follow a case that weaves throughout the upcoming pages that will not only help resolve the mystery surrounding the various social media entities that can facilitate learning in ways that are both practical and captivating but also demonstrate direct application in a student distance, problem-based learning (PBL) project.

The Case

Faculty commonly set aside time after teaching a class and evaluate what was done well and what could have been done better. When pausing for reflection, an instructor may discover a need to attend a faculty development class to improve current skills or to learn new ones. This case will illustrate just such an incident.

The physical therapy department meeting is winding down, and the decision is for Alex to have the opportunity to provide the distance, online clinic class for the second time. Last year, Alex used the university's Course Management System, Blackboard, to deliver the course. As she reflects back, she remembers the difficulty of balancing the need to maintain the students' interest with meeting the course's learning objectives. This uncomfortable experience led her to attend a series of faculty development classes offered by the university. The workshops focused on how to integrate social media into course curricula in hopes of gaining more tools for a professor's instructional toolbox. Alex sees this as an opportune time to find out if she can apply her newfound knowledge into her online class.

EMPOWERING PROBLEM-BASED
LEARNING WITH ONLINE SOCIAL MEDIA

The Tool: Online Social Media

A good place to begin this journey is with Web 2.0-driven online social media (OSM). Collis and Moonen (2008) define Web 2.0 as an enhanced focus on the use of Internet tools in order to collaborate, communicate, and distribute information. What may not be common knowledge is there were no true updates to Web 1.0; however, in 2004, user demands of the World Wide Web indicated the need to create the *Web 2.0* terminology (Collis & Moonen, 2008). Table 1.1 lists examples of tools and the accompanying instructional strategy/educational uses that Web 2.0 has brought to center stage (Franklin & van Harmelen, 2007). There are many other types of OSM that also provide authentic, educational experiences that lack representation in Table 1.1. To list them all would be an act of futility, as the list

TABLE 1.1. Examples of Web 2.0 Tools and Instructional Strategies

Social Media Category	Tools	Instructional Strategy/Educational Use
Communication	Facebook, LinkedIn, MySpace	Instructor posts lecture notes; students complete group homework; peer review of online reflections
Collaboration	Wikis	Platform for group work where individuals in the group can collaborate on a project; edit and have a running commentary on the progress of the project
	Blogs	Instructors use blogs for announcements and running dialogue with student questions; learners have the capability to provide comments on posts
	Social bookmarking	Students can bookmark web pages individually to create an aggregate of grouped pages to provide a resource in a specific area to further knowledge; may work as a group function for a project or entire course
Multimedia	Podcasts, YouTube, Flickr, Skype, VoiceThread, iTunes	Provides pre-lecture material, post-lecture replay to increase the depth of learning; tutorials or educational videos; interactive group presentation and feedback
Virtual World	Second Life	Platform for online synchronous learning; enables group work without physically needing to be present in the same room; instructors can "meet" with students during virtual office hours

Note. Adapted from "Web 2.0 for Content for Learning and Teaching in Higher Education," by T. Franklin and M. van Harmelen, 2007. Retrieved from Joint Information Systems Committee website: http://www.jisc.ac.uk/media/documents/programmes/digitalrepositories/web2-content-learning-and-teaching.pdf seems to grow daily. With this in mind, finding the time and resources in order to bring this into the classroom appears to be a justifiable challenge. How will social media facilitate meeting course objectives and promote better student engagement? How difficult is it to implement these tools?

The Approach: Problem-Based Learning

With the first question in mind, a path to meeting goals and enhancing student learning experiences begins with the selection of a solid instructional approach. Discussing PBL in association with OSM will help clarify how both of these tasks can occur.

In order to embark in a healthy discussion about PBL, a consideration of constructivism must come first. Constructivism is an umbrella term that identifies construction of knowledge, as when the learner develops a personal understanding of their interaction with their environment (Cheaney & Ingebritsen, 2005). Constructivism came about in the 1980s, which started a revolutionary change in instructional delivery. No longer accepted was the *sage on the stage* where the instructor alone possessed the fountain of knowledge. The *guide on the side* instructor who facilitates learning through scaffolding and mentoring took their place. With this coaching style of teaching came PBL as an instructional approach of constructivism. Cheaney and Ingebritson (2005) found that PBL activates students' previous knowledge and restructures authentic, real-world problems. In addition, they also established that higher-order learning and knowledge construction take place in the online PBL environment. Anderson and Tredway (2009) validated that as students immerse themselves into a case they tend to transition into the role of stakeholder that enables both control and responsibility in the learning process. In this manner, instructors become more like facilitators who promote not only learning but also reflection and application of new knowledge.

When OSM Meets PBL

Now that a solid foundation in PBL and tools of social media exists, next will be a closer look at how these two entities can synergistically enhance student learning. More and more, there is a focus on success as a team versus as an individual in the healthcare environment. Disciplines can no longer exist in silos and still provide patient-centered care. As a team, the patient receives the best possible care due to receiving treatment as a whole person not as a "knee" or "hip." With education mirroring work environments, students benefit from the group emphasis in PBL, which facilitates student learning in a more authentic setting. What form will PBL take as the social media explosion continues? Using OSM such as wikis, blogs, or Skype allows PBL to take on extended dimensions. For example, in the work setting, a PBL approach could assist in prototyping the next generation of computerized artificial limbs, also known as *prostheses*. Imagine a healthcare conference proceeding where Adobe Connect links to a research team in Hong Kong who is leading a discussion on a potential issue with the prosthesis' capability to heel strike at higher running speeds. After examination of several case-based scenarios, physical therapists, physicians, and prosthetists could problem solve the issues and share findings. When taking this example into the classroom, a cohort of students could use a similar social media tool to link to another classroom using PBL to problem solve cases as an interdisciplinary team.

Fast forward to real-world considerations and reflect about the facts presented in the video, *Social Media Revolution* (Qualman, 2009). Facebook added over 100 million users in nine months. Wikipedia has over 13 million articles, with 78% in languages other than English. The number of iPod applications downloaded in just nine months was over one billion. Lastly, Google has over 34,000 searches per second. What do these statistics imply? Users of social media have carved out a preferred pattern of technology use. Yet, how does this translate into the classroom? We will begin with a look from the student viewpoint and then explore the instructor's role.

In a study by Ogan, Ozakca, and Groshek (2008), college students spent on average 4.4 hours on the Internet, daily. According to Facebook, 85% of all four-year university students had a Facebook account. Brown (2010) put forward that reaching out to learners in their preferred environment promoted a higher level of engagement. He stated that as students blog or update their status on Facebook, an opportunity arose for the development of social community and reflection. When students had the ability to be a part of a class community on Facebook, this enabled them to analyze critically their participation on the social network and what the implications were for these actions.

Another consideration is the learner's desire for immersion in the learning experience. In an interview, Chris Dede shared that learners have an opportunity for this when involved in games or simulations (Crow, 2010). Thus, due to learners' dedication to the use of the Internet, social networking sites, and immersion activities, they have a significant impact on preferred online learning formats.

Thus, the literature indicates that students are becoming more and more techno-savvy. Conversely, are educators keeping up? According to Collis and Moonen (2008), students are experiencing frustration as the use of social media is growing exponentially and yet higher education institutions are sadly lagging behind. What the students see is the use of OSM as a tremendous source of empowerment. They can share content, tag, revise, and present it again in a matter of minutes. However, when they come to the classroom, this possibility is rare.

So what can instructors do about it? Demonstration and integration of instructional strategies, an understanding of what it means to embed Web 2.0 into the instructional design, as well as workarounds will help paint the answer to this question. Collis and Moonen (2008) stated that instructors and students must learn how participation, contribution, and knowledge together create an enhanced educational environment. The authors further argued that scaffolding gradually reduces the instructor's role in the learning experience then facilitates a student's increasing ability to create their own learning artifacts. However, they also suggested that accreditation, copyright infringement, and intellectual property issues may arise (Collis & Moonen, 2008). However, there are several ways to circumvent most of these concerns. To begin, support for the instructors in the form of faculty development funding, instructional technology (IT) support, and software packages helps. In addition to this, encouraging the techno-savvy student to utilize this new technology within the guidelines of the institution can create a synergistic environment where both sets of stakeholders have an opportunity for success.

Returning to Crow's interview (Crow, 2010), Dede discussed that in education we tend to look for the silver bullet. He found in his experience that educators are inclined to look for the one best practice and desire for it to take care of all learners. He advocates instead that we develop an ecology of dissimilar teaching best practices to suit the different styles of learners. A good online experience will have as many as possible media opportunities. For example, in his classes students use wikis, asynchronous and synchronous discussions, streaming videos, and social bookmarking. At the beginning of the semester, the students learn how to use social bookmarking and then the students take control. They set up web bookmarks as they explore the internet and then Dede creates an RSS feed into the classroom. The professor then utilizes some of the bookmarked web pages as a part of the instruction for the class. Thus, through this activity, the students develop a sense of ownership and contribution to the course content as they participate in the instruction and learning in the class. This also assists the instructor as it provides a platform for a continuous cycle of updating course content. Thus, a win–win situation develops from increased student engagement to self-perpetuating current course materials.

RESOLVING THE CASE WITH OSM

So what does this mean? Using PBL with authentic situations and collaborative work, OSM can not only facilitate meeting course objectives but also promote renewed student commitment to learning. The bigger question becomes, how does an instructor go about implementing these tools? Taking a moment to go back to the case and look at how an OSM instrument can be put into place to not only set in motion a positive learning experience but to also support the professor in instruction.

Use of Facebook

As Alex returns to her office, she reflects back on the difficulties she had instructing the course last year and prepares a mental list. The first barrier she ran into was that the students would rarely check their emails. Urgent messages would go unanswered for up to a week. Weekly assignments only guaranteed a once-a-week spot check, which was not a satisfactory solution. As she pulls out the manual from the first workshop and blows the dust off to see if it holds any answers to her query, she reads the word, "Facebook." Is this the answer to getting students to stay tuned in with the course and the program?

Facebook is a controversial educational medium where the average account holder spends almost an hour a day (Eldon, 2009). Why not take advantage of this? If this is where your students are, why not go where they spend their time. Some would suggest it is too close to mixing business with pleasure. However, there is an overabundance of other types of forums occurring on Facebook that do not include the marketing of wares or the "friending" of strangers. Universities are on Facebook actively recruiting for students, posting videos, and developing large followings for their athletic programs. With this is mind, an instructor could use this same forum to get class work accomplished. Posting of lecture notes, peer feedback on reflection pieces, announcements, or sending urgent messages should be acceptable practice.

However, there is a small glitch in this thought process. Preliminary research from Kirshner and Karpinski (2010) implied that college students who have Facebook accounts have lower GPAs and spend fewer hours studying than students who do not have accounts. This finding has created quite a stir with supporters of social media use as a vehicle for learning. To put things in perspective, Young (2009) interviewed Karpinski, who recommended more exploratory research in this area would be necessary in order to establish firm conclusions that this initial research could not. Again, why would an instructor go to Facebook for delivery of course content when initial research results bring debate? Understand that technology needs to assist the learning, not be the center of it. If the course objectives suggest an OSM tool can create a preferred learning environment for the student, then the instructor has an opportunity to try a new venue at minimal risk. Poll the students at midterm and again at final to assess satisfaction with the course and perceived impact of performing course activities on Facebook. In the meantime, take advantage of the opportunity to post announcements, assign reflections, and require journaling with peer feedback as well as student posts on the course wall. The instructor could also set up chats with students who are having difficulty or would like further explanation of the day's assignments. All of these prospects lie ahead for the instructor who gives Facebook a chance to cultivate a new venue for education.

Use of Wikis

Let us go back to the case and see how Alex's next obstacle reveals itself.

Alex believes that the utilization of Facebook is one step that she can take to get students to "come to class" in a distance format more often than before. This thought is outside her comfort zone, but she is determined to try new tools in order to deliver a better course this year. Looking at the next barrier on her list of challenges from last year is group projects. This was a significant issue. The group pages function in Blackboard was nice to share documents among students but did not provide the flexibility of prompt editing. It became frustrating not only for the students but for Alex as well. Recently, one of the other faculty members started using a wiki for group projects. She made an appointment to talk with this instructor to see how it was working for him.

So, what is a wiki and how can it help? A wiki is essentially an internet platform that enables its users to collaboratively work together to produce an artifact that may be publicly viewed or for individual groups only. This platform takes the form of a web page or multiple web pages whose properties may include text, images, sound, video, and so on (Farmer, 2006). It arguably lends itself to social constructivism where knowledge construction occurs in a group environment. Ward Campbell developed the first known wiki back in 1995 (Bold, 2006). His wiki was called WikiWikiWeb, which eventually became known as the Portland Pattern Repository.

Wikis have multiple purposes. Uses of a wiki include a place to brainstorm, meeting planning, research collaboration, planning conferences, instruction, project development, and writing collaborative reports (Lamb, 2004). A more recent application that has the attention of researchers is creating *wikibooks*. A case study by Ravid, Kalman, and Rafaeli (2008) shared their experiences in developing a wikibook over the course of two years as a collaborative effort between faculty and undergraduate and graduate students. The end product had over 564 sub-chapters. The authors reported a surge of empowerment because this online collaboration created a strong sense of community and academic performance of the students involved in the project.

A significant concern of novice wiki users is the idea of someone else being able to denigrate original work with revisions, feedback, and overall criticism that can be difficult for an ego to handle (Lamb, 2004). Once more experience is gained, the user can find it extremely helpful to get insights from colleagues. This provides a chance for development of outcomes that would not have been achievable by an individual effort.

The last trepidation with respect to wikis to cover is organization and aesthetic concerns. The organization of the usual wiki comes across a bit chaotic; however, underneath its rough exterior lies a plan. Most wikis have established guidelines. For instance, some guidelines include non-anonymous postings; permissions to add web pages; and no slang, vulgar images or curse words. The overall standard wiki appearance tends to lack the nice continuity of colors and formatting that other websites enjoy. This is an accepted dimension for wiki users; what a wiki lacks in beauty, it can make up for in functionality (Lamb, 2004).

The next consideration is how this plays out as a tool for interactive instruction. There are three main purposes in regards to its educational uses (Lamb, 2004). First, the wiki may exist as a student-only site to create communication within or across cohorts. It can also be a repository for a collection of works so that students and faculty members can do one-stop shopping. Finally, it may act as a support to writing instruction. Wikis have the potential to be invaluable for teaching writing skills, enhancing critical thinking, and facilitating autonomy. Lamb (2004) believes wikis have the capability to create *networking literacy* where the student can learn to write in a distributed, shared environment. As wikis invade educational settings, it may facilitate instructors coming out of the traditional ways of teaching more easily.

Wikis tend to be a flexible, versatile platform that prompts instructors to use it for projects that require a high amount of interactivity (Gazda & Hrabe, 2005). In this format, instructors are able to view projects as they progress from beginning to completion. They are also able to handle large documents where some course management systems cannot. Dlouha and Dlouhy (2010) state that wikis provide transparency for students and faculty which results in a non-competitive environment that promotes an easier venue for scaffolding. Taking this into consideration, Bold (2006) desired to utilize a wiki in her distance nursing class and understood that her students had concerns about using a wiki as most of them did not know HTML code. In her approach, she provided on the wiki introductory web pages, a quick "how-to" guide that explained the very basic codes needed to be able to participate fully in the wiki for her class. This went over very well with the students and the use of the wiki facilitated successful learning outcomes. The example implies that anxiety concerns that come with not having a working knowledge of HTML diminish with instructional support. This is not as commonly known as wiki designers would like. In fact, some wikis do not require any HTML coding at all.

To go one step further, the other side of the coin also needs examination, which is the side of the students. Student responses on the use of wikis for the most part have been positive. The perception exists that the technology promotes a conduit for a better sense of connectedness to other students and faculty (Bold, 2006). Students suggest that having high-speed internet access and a PC that has the current software systems should be standard in order to participate fully in wiki-based projects. Although students initially voice concerns about revising each other's work publicly, this seems to be overcome with the appropriate instructor mentoring and having a "sandbox wiki" to practice in first (Gazda & Hrabe, 2005).

To conclude, wikis can be a powerful tool for instructors and students alike. They are very appealing as they make it easy to author content, have open access, and possess unrestricted collaboration (Lamb, 2004). What is important to recognize is that choosing the right wiki includes making decisions about clearly defining what the purpose is for your project, who the users will be, does it need to be public or private, and what guidelines need to be in place knowing that the more guidelines instituted the increased likelihood for less creativity exists. In closing, the wiki prayer summarizes what wikis are all about...

> *Please, grant me the serenity to accept the pages I cannot edit,*
> *The courage to edit the pages I can,*
> *And the wisdom to know the difference.*
> *—The Wiki Prayer (Lamb, 2004)*

Use of Flickr, VoiceThread, and Skype

Now that the issues of poor email use and how to facilitate group work have been tackled, an exploration of multimedia in online social tools leads to the next issue to unravel in the case.

> *The semester has now begun and the online clinic class is up and running. Alex has chosen to require the students to post reflections on Facebook and provide peer feedback on fellow students' reflections. This is a new assignment for the students in the physical therapy program so they are now attempting to adjust to this innovative approach to meeting their course requirements. In addition, a group project assignment posted on Facebook today provides the students in clinic an opportunity to dive into a PBL case study in small groups depending upon the setting they are currently working.*
>
> *As future practicing physical therapists, they will encounter patients who will test their knowledge base and skill sets. Seizing the chance to learn how to solve this type of patient issue under the mentorship of a clinical instructor is invaluable to students' development and further authenticates their ability to become entry-level therapists. By using groups, Alex has provided an additional layer of PBL instruction. The students can work together to benefit from the knowledge that other clinical instructors possess, and the more advanced students can provide mentorship to the students who may need more help.*
>
> *The assignment's main objectives are to promote critical thinking, communication skills, and evidence-based practice. The problem presented to the groups is that each student must look at the most commonly occurring patient diagnosis treated in their clinic, examine the standard treatment regimen provided to this specific patient population, and find the evidence to support it. A wiki for each group will act as the platform for presentation of the information gleaned in this process. The group will then decide which treatment regimen has the most and the least evidence to support it for one given*

diagnosis. At this point, the group will subdivide into two teams where they will follow one of the two chosen cases and chronicle a patient's progression in clinic. Alex recommends that a pictorial representation will assist the other groups in understanding how the patients improve over time. The final product will be an online presentation outlining the decision process, patient progress, and a comparison to the guidelines of standard practice demonstrating which patient treatment regimen enabled a faster and effective return to the prior level of function.

The decision to use the wiki is simple since, in order to have the flexibility of group revisions and feedback, the wiki is an ideal option. Although the choice of including pictures of patients, with their permission of course, would allow the students in the other clinics to see how the patients are advancing with the physical therapy interventions, it does require yet another decision of what is the best means of expression for sharing this presentation.

A picture is worth a thousand words. As the students in the case consider which of their peers has the best series of patient progression photos, what will be the best OSM tool in which to present the pictures of the final product? One option is using Flickr. This multimedia site would allow the uploading of pictures as well as tagging the picture so that the students could look at the chronicling of a patient's progress over time. Unfortunately, it does not have the capability to present the photos and promote "in the moment" interaction with the rest of the class.

An alternative choice to consider would be VoiceThread. This OSM tool enables multiple users to have a conversation about documents, graphics, or videos. The participants can communicate via microphone, webcam, telephone, or text. The speaker can actually draw on the main frame image as they are talking to emphasize the portion of the graphic to which he or she is referring. Figure 1.1 is a screen shot that illustrates how this tool works. A participant is drawing a circle around the dragon's tail as he is discussing the topic at hand. Note that while he is speaking, a megaphone symbol denotes it is his turn; however, other participants can be writing their comments and then the text appears for all participants to see when the speaker is finished. This typed feedback would be in a dialogue box similar to the megaphone symbol. The small picture icons on either side of the image that run along the left and right borders represent of all of the participants in the conference. Each student is able to see the image and each other's icons. They are able to comment, as they desire to do so. The editor of the call has an additional ability where he or she may select the best comments and allow only those to be visible to all of the participants.

Along with the variety of communication options, VoiceThread has multiple characteristics that promote its use for this type of collaboration. One of the best features of this tool is that it possesses the capability of recording a meeting so that it can become an artifact for the class in which all of the members can review at their convenience. It also supports imports of

FIGURE 1.1.   This screenshot represents a moment in time of a collaborative meeting that is taken from a demonstration within the VoiceThread website. Note that not only is there spoken word occurring, but also a circle is being drawn around the tail so as to bring the participants' attention to the area the speaker is emphasizing (What's a VoiceThread Anyway, 2010).

photos from both Flickr and Facebook. This multimedia device promotes both communications and feedback simultaneously. Thus, VoiceThread is a solid solution; however, when requiring this type of assignment, significant issues can arise.

> *Notably, when an introduction of a new group project occurs, it is imperative to insure the ability to provide feedback for any needs for clarification from the students. Indeed, this is what happens when one of the groups would like to talk to Alex face to face but are unable to do so as they are scattered across the country. This leads Alex to, once again, pull the handouts from the faculty development classes she attended and contemplates what would be the best channel for communication with her students.*

What is the best way to handle the concern of how to best meet with the students who are asking for clarification of the assignment? An instant chat can occur on Facebook or on Blackboard. A conference call could work, but it would not allow either the instructor or the students to visually see each other. A video teleconference could be a good solution to this predicament. Skype is an OSM tool that can fulfill this need. Traditionally, it allowed two people to connect and have video/audio interface. However, in May 2010, Skype successfully piloted video-conferencing for up to 10 people. Thus, this medium would allow the students in the group to be able to see and hear their instructor and vice versa. This type of forum is an extremely valuable communication device, as each person on the call can not only hear the verbal interactions but also observe the nonverbal gestures of the rest of the callers in order to gain a better understanding of the discussion.

Use of a Virtual World

Several Skype meetings resulted in the clarifying of directions, validating the chosen patients, and review of presentations. The online class is beginning to wind down. However, there is one final wrinkle to address in the case.

The VoiceThread student presentations went well. Each group presented their findings on the patient cases. To their surprise, they were able to expertly defend their choices of best and least evidence-based treatment regimens. They demonstrated critical thinking and ability to search the evidence accurately. The environment created by the PBL experience necessitated an increase in communication skills among students, clinical instructors, and patients in the face-to-face and online venues. Yet there was a missing communicative component uncovered. Upon review of the students' case studies, a common theme emerged where the students markedly were having difficulty with understanding how the interdisciplinary team works together, especially for discharge planning. This is a critical piece. Physical therapists must work in concert with other healthcare professionals in order to promote a holistic approach to be able to reach enhanced patient outcomes.

Alex's college has recently developed an island in Second Life®, an online virtual world, that houses healthcare disciplines. She decides to contact her fellow faculty members to see if they would be interested in participating in a group education event where the students would go on a "scavenger hunt." This would occur by having the students gather artifacts from each virtual interdisciplinary instructor after they had presented discipline-specific information on how their specific role on the healthcare team plays out especially with discharge planning. By the end of the hunt, the students will have constructed a "whole patient" as well as the knowledge they need in order to provide a better discharge experience for their future patients in clinic.

How does Second Life® work and does it possess the potential to facilitate accelerated student engagement (Second Life, 2010)? To begin by taking a step back to look at the bigger picture, a common saying that comes to mind when talking about emerging technologies is, "People's perceptions are their own realities." Furthermore, the tendency can be to run towards innovation as Reiser (2007) shares, or it can be to run from it. Innovation in and of itself can create misperceptions that are born of ignorance, especially when it comes to technology as it relates to computers. Sam, Othman, and Nordin (2005) discuss how computer self-efficacy can greatly affect a person's ability to perform computer tasks. The fear of touching the wrong key on a computer keyboard can be terrifying, so much so that it becomes a self-fulfilling prophecy. Considering the ominous mix of the fear of computers, adding in the snowball effect of the increased use of distance learning and virtual worlds yields the creation of the perfect storm.

At the center of this storm are virtual worlds. Recreational use was at one time, the primary function of virtual worlds but they have now evolved into ever-expanding learning environments (Dickey, 2006). To get a better understanding of what Second Life® is, the introduction page from their website explains:

> Second Life® is a 3D virtual world created by its Residents that's bursting with entertainment, experiences, and opportunity. Second Life® provides the platform where the Second Life® world resides and offers the tools for business, educators, nonprofits, and entrepreneurs to develop a virtual presence. Headquartered in San Francisco, Linden Lab has over 330 employees spread across the U.S., Europe, and Asia. (Second Life, 2010, n.p.)

Phillip Rosedale, in 1999, created Second Life®, which is maintained by Linden Lab. Second Life® has grown from having 2 million to 13 million residents from 2003 to 2006 (Shen & Eder, 2009). This virtual world has its own economy with the Linden dollar as the monetary unit. Objects, office space, and entire islands exist in this world. Its uses currently expand beyond recreational activity boundaries into an ever-growing popularity with educational endeavors.

As with any online tool, it has both strengths and weaknesses. The strengths of a virtual environment depend upon the perception of the person using it. Second Life® gives learners control and choice. Students find the 3D environment not only more interesting but fun. Having the ability to self-pace, explore, build objects, and visit locations across the globe without leaving the desktop computer can be a priceless experience. Another strength Second Life® possesses is its anonymity, which can be powerful for some students. A student who is passive in the traditional classroom can experience the feeling of freedom when in the virtual world. Learners can design an avatar that looks like themselves or nothing at all. They can pick clothes, decorate a space, and most importantly be more open to experiences with other students in the class under the veil of their avatar.

Additional Second Life® strengths concentrate on virtual world versus real world. Real-life issues in general are less likely to arise. As with any distance class, a snow day is not a problem. Traffic does not cause someone to be late in the virtual environment. Good planning and potential asynchronous assignments allow tasks to be accomplished when the student has time to get it done. Lastly, distance, hybrid model, and traditional classes have an opportunity for students to collaborate in a way that has not been available before. Class projects allow students across the globe to work together to problem solve, build communities, exchange economic ideas, and so on. Its uses are limited only to one's imagination (Research Linden Lab, 2009).

Aside from the student advantages, instructors have additional benefits. Instructors can have virtual office hours to meet with students but are able to do so from any physical location of their choosing. The instructor may also facilitate student "study buddies," and promote the use of video and audio playback of lectures (Shen & Eder, 2009). With these characteristics in mind, Second Life® can provide a rich, innovative virtual world learning environment that is beneficial to both the student and the instructor.

As previously stated, the thought of utilizing Second Life® as a virtual world playground for adults has been around since its inception. However, looking at Second Life® as a collegiate environment is a more current concept. In this virtual world, companies are holding meetings, and universities and professional organizations are creating entire islands. For example, the Association for Educational Communications and Technology (AECT) launched CAVE Island in October of 2009. AECT is using Second Life® as a platform for participating in virtual world events, developing and uploading content, and networking among colleagues (*AECT_SL C.A.V.E. Island*, 2009). This is just one of many organizations that have taken advantage of the features Second Life® has to offer.

However, if there are strengths in the virtual world learning environment, then there are sure to be pitfalls. Fear is one of the biggest downsides of Second Life®. Fear of pushing the wrong button, getting lost, acting in an

FIGURE 1.2.   This image comes from the introduction webpage of Second Life®. It demonstrates an example of how avatars can interact as they enter into a meeting. Second Life® (2010). In Second Life® website. Retrieved from: http://secondlife.com/

abnormal manner in front of other avatars are just a few of the concerns of a novice user. Outside of the user, not all computers support the expansive technological requirements of the Second Life® program.

How does the downside relate to education? Tapping into the imagination thought process, a significant hurdle lies with the instructor. Can an instructor utilize this environment across various subject matter areas? If the content is economics, engineering, or teacher education, the application may work, but what if the topic relates to healthcare education? Can a nurse, physical therapist, or physician have quality learning experiences utilizing Second Life®? Regan and Youn (2008) suggest that the best way to teach clinical skills is through a hybrid environment. Second Life® can facilitate learning, but face-to-face time with an instructor for the hands-on experience has its place as well.

Therefore, imagination and hurdles provide the outline for the educational implications and learning experiences that are available in Second Life®. The learning possibilities are endless, but as with any other innovation, keeping the technology as a catalyst for learning and not as a "parlor trick" will allow true learning to occur. This takes us back to where we started with the effort to untangle misperceptions about virtual world learning. Thus, as with any learning tool there continues to be a need to perform research to validate the various types of educational methodologies that can occur within virtual worlds.

CONCLUSION

Taking a moment to reflect on learning objectives, student engagement, and the ever-advancing social media technology, we can see that multiple challenges lie ahead in integrating the use of OSM into the classroom. First, it is important to remove the mystery surrounding OSM. To know that Web 2.0 does not mean that an actual update to the Internet occurred helps in removing some of the anxiety that may accompany OSM. Second, there is potential for a frustrating gap to exist between the student and instructor. Why would we, as educators, lose an opportunity to grasp our students' attention and enhance their learning in a format that is familiar to them? We can see where some material may naturally lend itself to different multimedia tools whereas some material may not. However, if the content does not cooperate, then why not provide a venue for the students to communicate outside of class to further learning.

With these questions asked and answered, it is also important to note that if the institution does not support new faculty development in this area it is difficult to get these ideas off the ground. In addition to institutional backing, the instructor has to have an open mind to learning how to use these new tools in order to enhance students' learning experiences. Through utilization of the case throughout the chapter, we hope the implementation of these tools is clearer and yields an understanding that it is not a difficult endeavor to conquer but it is an intentional venture to come to the edge, meet the students on their terms, and leap from obsolete to trendy.

REFERENCES

AECT_SL C.A.V.E. Island. (2009). Training and Performance AECT Division. [Brochure].

Anderson, G., & Tredway, C. (2009). Transforming the nursing curriculum to promote critical thinking online.*Journal of Nursing Education,48*(2),111–5. doi:1635327731

Bold, M. (2006). Use of wikis in graduate course work. *Journal of Interactive Learning Research, 17*(1), 5–14.

Brown, A. (2010). Social media: A new frontier in reflective practice. *Medical Education, 44,* 744–745. doi: 10.1111/j.1365-2293.2010.03729.x

Cheaney, J., & Ingebritsen, T. S. (2005). Problem-based learning in an online course: a case study. *International Review of Research in Open and Distance Learning, 6*(3), 1–18.

Collis, B., & Moonen, J. (2008). Web 2.0 tools and processes in higher education: quality perspectives. *Educational Media International, 45*(2), 93–106.

Crow, T. (2010). Learning, no matter where you are. *Journal of Staff Development, 31*(1), 10–17.

Dickey, M. (2006). Girl gamers: The controversy of girl games and the relevance of female-oriented game design for instructional design. *British Journal of Educational Technology, 37*(5), 785–793.

Dlouha, J., & Dlouhy, J. (October, 2010). Use of wiki tools for raising the communicate aspect of learning. Presented at the 7th European Conference on e-Learning, Agia Napa.

Eldon, R. (2009, December 2). Facebook's own statistics show content-sharing increase, new status-update trends, and more [Web log post]. Retrieved from http://www.insidefacebook.com/2009/12/02/facebooks-own-statistics-show-content-sharing-increase-new-status-update-trends-and-more/

Farmer, R. (2006). Wiki—An effective collaborative learning tool. *Journal of Interactive Instruction Development, 19*(1), 3–7.

Franklin, T., & van Harmelen, M. (2007). Web 2.0 for content for learning and teaching in higher education. Retrieved from Joint Information Systems Committee website: http://www.jisc.ac.uk/media/documents/programmes/digitalrepositories/web2-content-learning-and-teaching.pdf

Gazda, R., & Hrabe, D. (2005). Wikis as an instructional tool: Feat or failure. *Journal of Instructional Delivery Systems, 22*(1), 12–17.

Kirshner, P., & Karpinski, A. (2010). Facebook and academic performance. *Computers in Human Behavior, 26,* 1237–1245. doi: 10.1016/j.chb.2010.03.024

Lamb, B. (2004). Wide open spaces wikis ready or not. *Educause Review, 36,* 38–48.

Ogan, C., Ozakca, M., & Groshek, J. (2008). Embedding the internet in the lives of college students: Online and offline behavior. *Social Sciences Computer Review, 26*(2), 170–177. doi: 10.1177/0894439307306129

Qualman, E. *(*2009). Social media revolution: Is social media a fad? Available from http://www.youtube.com/watch?v=sIFYPQjYhv8

Ravid, G., Kalman, Y.M., & Rafaeli, S. (2008). Wikibooks in higher education: empowerment through online distributed collaboration. *Computers in Human Behavior, 24,* 1913–1928, doi: 10.1016/j.chb. 2008.02.010

Regan, J., & Youn, E. (2008). Past, present, and future trends in teaching clinical skills through web-based learning environments. *Journal of Social Work Education, 44*(2), 95–114.

Reiser, R. A. (2007). A history of instructional design and technology. In R. A. Reiser & J. V. Dempsey (Eds.), *Trends and issues in instructional design and technology* (pp. 18–28). Englewood Cliffs, NJ: Merrill Prentice Hall.

Research Linden Lab. (2009). Retrieved from http://lindenlab.com/ Sam, H. K., Othman, A. E. A., & Nordin, Z. S. (2005). Computer self-efficacy, computer anxiety, and attitudes toward the Internet: A study among undergraduates in Unimas. *Educational Technology & Society, 8*(4), 205–219.

Second Life. (2010). In Second Life® website. Retrieved from: http://secondlife.com/

Second Life Research. (2009). Retrieved from http://secondliferesearch.blogspot.com

Shen, J., & Eder, L.B. (2009). Intentions to use virtual worlds for education. *Journal of Information Systems Education, 20*(2), 225–233.

What's a VoiceThread Anyway. (2010). In VoiceThread website. Retrieved from http://voicethread.com/?#q

Young, J. (2009). Facebook, grades, and media hype hype. *The Chronicle of Higher Education, 55*(33), 13.

UNIT 2

K-12 APPLICATION

CHAPTER 2

RETWEETING HISTORY

Exploring the Intersection of Microblogging and Problem-based Learning for Historical Reenactments

Victor R. Lee, Brett E. Shelton, Andrew Walker, Tom Caswell, and Marion Jensen

Historical reenactments are an activity in which history enthusiasts research historical figures and gather to act out a famous historical event as those individuals. This chapter describes a development and implementation framework for conducting historical reenactments virtually using the Twitter microblogging service. Following a general introduction to the practices associated with historical reenactment, we describe the steps involved in successfully organizing a virtual reenactment, share some examples from already completed virtual reenactments, and present a firsthand retrospective and reflection from a high school teacher who led her history students in a virtual reenactment of the Cuban Missile Crisis. We discuss some central challenges associated with aligning virtual reenactments to problem-based learning approaches and close with specific proposals for improvements that could be made in future implementations.

Designing Problem-Driven Instruction with Online Social Media, pages 23–40

INTRODUCTION

History educators have increasingly been focused on finding ways to involve students in authentic practices associated with professionals who study and interpret the discipline of history (Hynd, Holschuh, & Hubbard, 2004; Spoehr & Spoehr, 1994; Wiley & Voss, 1996; Wineburg, 2001). This more practice-based approach to history teaching is motivated in part by calls made in recent standards documents (National Center for History in the Schools, 1996) and also by the belief that authentic activities mirroring the work done by professionals can result in more robust learning (Brown, Collins, & Duguid, 1989; Wineburg, 2001). It is our view that newly emerging web technologies may provide an important new access point for students to participate in historical practices. For instance, the Internet is democratizing access to historical records and artifacts (Bass, Rosenzweig, & Mason, 1999). That access makes it possible for nearly anyone to work with and examine primary source materials from major historical events. Given the development of this new informational infrastructure along with the push toward development of authentic learning activities, we believe the time is ripe for considering ways in which new web-based tools and problem-based learning (PBL) principles can be combined to create an environment that promotes student interpretation of historical events. Specifically, we believe social media practices, like microblogging (Nardi, Schiano, Gumbrecht, & Swartz, 2004), could play a key role. This chapter describes a development and implementation framework for integrating microblogging and historical reenactment in a service called TwHistory.[1] In the sections below, we describe the TwHistory program, present an example from a high school classroom, and provide one teacher's report of the experience of using TwHistory. We then consider ways in which what we have developed adheres to the core commitments of problem-based learning and offer some suggestions for how virtual historical reenactments could be designed in the future with additional alignment to PBL design principles.

HISTORICAL REENACTMENTS AND THE SELECTION OF AUTHENTIC PROBLEMS

Due to its documented efficacy across a wide range of disciplines and types of assessment (Gijbels, Dochy, Van den Bossche, & Segers, 2005; Walker & Leary, 2009), PBL has garnered a great deal of interest among a diverse set of scholars from various disciplines (Savery, 2006). PBL has been paired with other various interventions and formats such as collaborative learning (Nelson, 1999) and educational games (Walker & Shelton, 2008), and it is seeing emerging use in K–12 settings (Ertmer & Simons, 2006). Since its inception in medical education (Barrows, 1996), the term "problem-based learning" has been adapted and changed (Barrows, 1986) to meet

the needs of various disciplines and contexts. Yet, despite the promising results of PBL across several content areas, development of PBL experiences
for social sciences has been relatively limited.[2]

Given the limited research landscape, there is additional preparatory
work that must be done to create a history-oriented PBL learning experience with new web 2.0 technologies. That is, it is necessary first and foremost to carefully select facets of history as a discipline that make sense for
a PBL instructional approach. We must consider, for instance, the kinds
of authentic problems faced by those with expert knowledge of history,
the skills that separate those individuals from traditional history students,
and scenarios that allow students to take on relevant roles. While there are
many possibilities (Gallagher & Stepien, 1996), we have chosen to focus
on *historical reenactment* and its related activity of *historical perspective taking*.
Taken together, these activities require individuals to examine and evaluate
historical documents and assume the role of a participant in a set of practices (Lave & Wenger, 1991) that centrally involve the gathering of relevant
historical evidence.

Historical reenactment is an activity undertaken typically by historians and
history enthusiasts who have studied an event and wish to simulate it with others. For example, enthusiasts may gather to simulate the Battle of Gettysburg
or an extended 1770 sea voyage of the *Endeavour* (Cook, 2004). For the reenactment to work, a high level of coordination is required: Participants must
schedule activities, establish character relationships, and assign key lines to
be said by various actors. While reenactment is typically recreational, hobby-
ists often research their roles passionately. This research typically requires
historical perspective taking, in which one must review available informational resources in order to determine the values, obligations, mannerisms,
social influences, and customs associated with individuals of a time period.
Understanding these perspectives is necessary as it helps historians and history enthusiasts to understand why particular individuals or groups of people
behaved or acted in the ways that they did for a given time.

Echoes of Other Instructional Approaches

It is worth noting that both reenactment and perspective taking are, at
least to some extent, reminiscent of other instructional approaches, such
as role-play or simulations. Approaches involving the use of role-play within historical educational realms have been advocated as one way to learn
about perspectives of different individuals in historical situations (McDaniel, 2000). This is in part because role play offers students a way of considering viewpoints that forces context when producing, or thinking about
reproducing, historical voices. Simulations, on the other hand, are considered a step beyond most role play kinds of activity structures in that they
often include a more rigid set of circumstances in which the context takes

place, they include an important set of objectives as directed by a facilitator or instructor, and they are less often accompanied by models that help form and affect the structure of the exercise (Hertel & Millis, 2002; Jones, 1987). Originally, role play was designed with the assumption of face-to-face interactions between participants. Of course, simulations of the most recent decades are associated with technological support of some kind, whether that support comes as part of behavior or environment models. Modern-day simulations may offer virtual means for communication between simulation participants. Virtual 3D worlds such as Second Life, or other forms of multi-user virtual environments, have been used to offer learning means that can enable role play but also take advantage of affordances simulations inherently offer (Davison & Gordon, 1978; Shelton & Wiley, 2007). For example, teachers can offer areas for students to practice in situations that would normally be too expensive or too difficult to reproduce using real-world means. These environments can also be made available to students learning asynchronously or living in geographically diverse places.

In consideration of the potential to engage in role play and simulation with the aid of social media, virtual communications between participants are also featured prominently. What is perhaps unique about social media compared to traditional views of role play and simulation is the public nature of the interactions. For example, students learning through social media now have the opportunity to send and receive messages in asynchronous and public formats, which may alter the parameters of the exercise and require some reconsideration on how the design of effective learning simulations may be most effectively produced and implemented. This holds true for virtual historical reenactments.

TWITTER AS A REENACTMENT ENVIRONMENT

As stated above, we are particularly interested in using social media, and in particular, the Twitter microblogging platform, for our work. By using Twitter, it is possible to move historical reenactments into a virtual space rather than a physical one. The virtual space is an attractive alternative for reenactments that take place over the course of many days or weeks. Participants are still posed with the challenges associated with gathering evidence in order to "act the part," and they must also coordinate actions and events with others. For students, particularly of the college and high school ages, we think that moving to an online reenactment environment is an especially appropriate step to take. New media have created many new opportunities for youth engagement in the disciplines (Jenkins, 2009). A Pew Internet and American life survey found that half of all American teens and 57% of teens who use the Internet could be considered content creators. These teens have created a blog, web page, or posted other content online (Lenhart & Madden, 2005). Not only are the tools available for positioning students as content creators, but also they are able and willing to use them. The opportunity for educators is to engage students in a topic that may not initially interest them by using new media that does, by treating students as practitioners of history, and by adopting principles from PBL to create an engaging and authentic learning environment.

Twitter is a relatively well-known microblogging technology in which messages, or tweets, are sent and received from these user profiles through varying protocols, and mostly viewed through computers and hand-held devices. As with other types of microblogs, tweets are often of a personal nature, involving commentary or description of one's activities and one's opinions about some current state of affairs (Nardi et al., 2004). Twitter is unique, relative to other microblogging services in that it imposes a 140-character maximum for tweets. Originally, this had been set as part of an effort to ensure compatibility with Simple Message Syndication (SMS) texting systems, but this constraint has remained even though texting technologies have advanced beyond the initial character limit.

TwHistory was implemented first in early 2009 with virtual historical reenactments of the Battles of Chancellorsville and Gettysburg that took place over a period of two months. Rather than ask actors to gather in a designated place, the first group of participants in this program instead used Internet collaboration tools to set up Twitter profiles for the characters they

 Harpers_Weekly Gen. Meade's troops were placed in order, and charged down the hill and into the town.
7:13 PM Jul 3rd from Tweet Master

 AD_Betts Col. Bennett wounded. Lieut. Connell, of Co. G., killed.
5:58 PM Jul 3rd from Tweet Master

 Col_wainwright Some of my men rode to where the battle took place. They tell me the ground is covered with dead.
5:23 PM Jul 3rd from Tweet Master

 Harpers_Weekly Leaving dead and wounded behind them, the enemy's forces slowly retreated upon their own hill and into their woods again.
5:13 PM Jul 3rd from Tweet Master

 John_Apperson The wounded are pouring in.
3:38 PM Jul 3rd from Tweet Master

 Dunn_Browne The fighting is not done yet, but we hope for the best and for a glorious Fourth tomorrow.
3:36 PM Jul 3rd from Tweet Master

FIGURE 2.1. Screenshot of Twitter feed from the Gettysburg reenactment.

would be playing. Events would be documented through tweets that could be directed to other character profiles (indicated by the "@" character followed by a profile name). Followers of Twitter reenactments received tweets in real time as the characters of a particular historical event reported from their perspective about what was happening. In the original Gettysburg reenactment, generals, citizens, soldiers, and even Abraham Lincoln had profiles from which tweets reporting the events of the battle were sent out. A sample set of tweets in a feed is shown in Figure 2.1.

The TwHistory Gettysburg reenactment drew a diverse set of followers who subscribed to the Twitter feeds. One of the Gettysburg followers was a very enthusiastic and skilled high school teacher located in the Midwest region of the United States, whom we refer to as Ms. F. With assistance from two of the authors (Tom Caswell and Marion Jensen), Ms. F. adapted the TwHistory model to create a Twitter-based reenactment of the Cuban Missile Crisis as part of a Cold War History course she was teaching, using a version of the development and implementation framework described in the section below.

BUILDING A TWHISTORY REENACTMENT

Developing a reenactment requires, first and foremost, the selection of a major historical event. Once such an historical event has been selected, the virtual reenactment development framework consists of four steps: Role assignment, content creation, content sequencing, and deployment. First, participants identify key historical figures in the historical event. After the cast of historical characters is set, assignments are made regarding which individual or individuals will research which character. In the classroom, this would ideally involve a group of three to four students assigned to a single character. Depending on classroom size, this can be varied to meet the needs of the historical event and the size of the class. For other populations, such as adult history enthusiasts, it is entirely possible to have a single person play one or even multiple roles.

In the second step, the content is researched, evaluated, and discussed using available web resources and print materials provided by the teacher or facilitator. The small group configuration that we recommend for the classroom, in which single characters are played jointly be multiple students, is intended to promote discussion about where to search for appropriate information on the historical figure, encourage group reflection on the quality and relevance of the historical information that is found, and support team-based decision making about how to incorporate the information into the reenactment. Doing this work provides opportunities for students to engage in some of the same cognitive work as historians. Once a small group is in agreement about what to portray and how, the tweets are written and stored in a separate file until sequencing is determined.

The 140-character constraint in tweets is seen as being advantageous for at least two reasons. First, it encourages students to be concise. They must find a way to synthesize and compactly summarize important ideas so they can fit within a single tweet. Second, the small length of tweets encourages more frequent posts and allows for inclusion of character "flourishes." Students have the opportunity when reenacting an event in TwHistory to consider and include seemingly mundane activities in the lives of their characters, as long as it is backed by historical evidence. For example, in a recent reenactment of the Mormon Pioneer Trek of 1848, historical records showed that one pioneer, Orson Pratt, regularly noted barometer readings each day of the journey. The TwHistory reenactment ultimately included a number of morning barometer reading tweets to reflect this documented activity. These flourishes allowed the enactor to share more about what he had learned about the trek and Orson Pratt, and also helped to convey to enactment followers some information about environmental conditions and routine activities of these historic individuals.

The third step in making a TwHistory reenactment involves the entire class or group of participants combining all the character tweets together in chronological order. This provides an opportunity for students to verify that participants have written appropriate tweets that fit properly with what other Twitter characters will be tweeting and determine if there are any holes that need to be filled. This is especially true when tweets must be timed to the exact minute. Often historical documents do not give an exact time for when an event occurred, so the reenactors must make their best guesses about the exact times. For the sake of maintaining a sequential flow of events, that guesswork is sufficient. However, some events need to be coordinated across characters for consistency. For example, several of the historical figures involved in the Battle of Gettysburg were also involved in Pickett's Charge. When the orders came to move, it needed to be uniform from both the characters involved in the march, as well as the Union soldiers who noted the charge had begun. In the classroom, this work of coordination and tweet sequencing represents an opportunity for students to shift their attention from interpreting the activities of an individual historical figure to a more explicit consideration of the events and interactions that they will be simulating. For other groups of learners and reenactors who do not share a classroom space, this coordination can be done asynchronously and remotely.

The final step is deployment. One option is for participants to manually send out tweets throughout the days of the reenactment at intermittent periods. However, for followers of the historical event, this has the potential of producing feeds that are hard to understand or situate within an actual timeline of events and decisions. For example, a haphazard character tweet about a diplomatic meeting with a government leader that takes place after tweets have been made indicating that the government leader had been assassinated would create unnecessary confusion. An alternative that we have explored is the use of a "cartridge" system in which the final set of tweets is written and loaded into a third-party service that will then "fire" the tweets at the same time of day in which the actual event took place.[3] While the decision to adhere to actual times ultimately is one that needs to be made by the class of students or by other, non-school-based participants in a reenactment, we consider the convenience of using a cartridge system to have a number of practical advantages. For a class of students, limitations of a rigid school schedule are easily overcome. Additionally, using a scheduler system creates a reflective learning opportunity for students as they observe the virtual events as they unfold and consider whether their collective interpretation and reenactment is indeed a coherent and accurate retelling of those events.

TWHISTORY IN THE CLASSROOM: AN EXAMPLE AND REFLECTION

During October of 2009, the aforementioned veteran social studies teacher, Ms. F., collaborated with two of the authors to lead a class of high school students through a multi-week process of reenacting the Cuban Missile Crisis. For the reenactment, the students played the roles of John F. Kennedy, Robert MacNamara, Nikita Khruschev, and Fidel Castro, among others. The students drew from materials they had received in class as well as primary sources obtained through the Library of Congress website. The students published over 500 tweets that began with Major Richard Heyser tweeting about preparations for his U-2 plane flight over Cuba and concluded with tweets from MacNamara and Kennedy reporting a peaceful resolution to the crisis and plans for the future.

After the reenactment, we engaged in a structured reflection with Ms. F. about her class and their experiences. As her firsthand account may prove useful for others who are considering creating their own TwHistory reenactments, we provide several of her responses below.[4]

> Researcher: Now that you have completed a historical reenactment using Twitter, would you do it again? Why or why not?
>
> Ms. F.: Definitely—the kids seemed to enjoy it, and by the end of it were really getting into character, although a few students complained about how "hard" it was to do all of the work necessary.
>
> Researcher: Looking back on this project, was the result what you expected? Were there any unexpected benefits or drawbacks?
>
> Ms. F.: I would have liked to see a little more discussion between the characters, but I think I needed to give the students more prep time—before the crisis actually began—in order for them to be

McGeorgeBundy The Soviets want to have a trade. We take our missiles out of Turkey and then they will take theirs out of Cuba...
10:00 AM Oct 27th from Tweet Master

RobMcNamara64 Just heard Radio Moscow broadcasting Khrushchev msg calling for us 2 pull missiles from Turkey. May need 2 compromise 2 achieve stability.
9:00 AM Oct 27th from Tweet Master

JFK_1962 now listening in on radio Moscow and @NikitaKhrushche speech. a little different from his letters that we have received in the past 2 days
9:00 AM Oct 27th from Tweet Master

FidelCastro62 battery of SAM missiles operated by Soviets fired+brought down U2 spy plane, pilot killed. People in Cuba very calm.
8:30 AM Oct 27th from Tweet Master

FidelCastro62 @NikitaKrushche , you should have told US that the Cubans should have been included in discussions: We are not opposed to a solution
8:15 AM Oct 27th from Tweet Master

FIGURE 2.2. Twitter feed excerpt from the high-school student-led reenactment of the Cuban Missile Crisis.

more fully prepared to have the sort of interaction that I discussed. In terms of overall results, however, it was what I expected, and the kids seem to have come out of it with a very good understanding of just what happened during the Cuban Missile Crisis.

Researcher: Now that you have done it once, what would you change?

Ms. F.: I needed to give them more prep time. Most of my students weren't familiar with Twitter, so I think I needed to give them more time to learn how it works, how to communicate in it, etc.

Researcher: What other resources do you think are needed for a historical reenactment using Twitter?

Ms. F.: I did provide a wiki for the class with a list of good websites that provided research information, as well as appropriate books, which I think was necessary. If my students were told to just find this info on their own, they would have been lost, but by giving them a series of eight to ten websites that gave them proper information/documentation/primary sources from the crisis, they were able to put together timelines.

Researcher: How much time did you spend on the Cuban Missile Crisis?

Ms. F.: It took a little more time than a normal unit. We devoted six days of in-class time for students to research and work on the project.

They also had homework for ten days that was dedicated specifically to this project. Overall, we started this project on October 12th, and ran it through October 28th. Of course, that includes a few days in between with other activities or lectures.

Researcher: Considering that it took longer than a normal unit, was it worth all the time the students spent to do this activity?

Ms. F.: I think it was worth the time. I had to sacrifice a little bit of content and, next year, when we go to a trimester schedule, will have to sacrifice more if I want to include this project, but I think it's valuable. While there were of course some students who seemed reluctant—as there always are for any activity—the majority seemed engaged and active. In particular, the groups who challenged themselves by taking on some of the larger roles/parts seemed to get the most out of it. They seemed invested and interested in making sure the project ran smoothly, which I was impressed by. Any time students take responsibility for making sure a lesson works, it's a good thing.

Researcher: In your opinion, did the Twitter reenactment encourage the development of any of curriculum specific skills?

Ms. F: Our curriculum specifies that students should work on research and writing. In particular, I think the reenactment helped with research. It was probably less so with writing. I had them turn in a short synopsis at the end, and based on that, I'm not sure that the project really helped their writing skills. But having them going through transcripts of White House meetings, or primary resources of any sort, was a very good thing, and I think made them think of these resources as accessible, and not the "big, frightening, intimidating sources" that most kids think of when they think of research with a primary source.

In summary, Ms. F. was generally positive about her experiences with TwHistory and believed it had specific benefits for students' reading activities. It generated a good amount of enthusiasm among students and only required a little more time than a unit she would normally teach. Also, establishing a set of common resources for students to reference was, in Ms. F.'s estimation, a very important contribution that she made as a teacher.

Based on these observations and our own reading of her class's virtual reenactment, we are optimistic that TwHistory can serve as an effective platform for students to engage in the problems associated with historical reenactment and perspective taking. As Ms. F. stated, many students "were really getting into character" as they gave voices to the characters they created. Yet, even with one case of a successful enactment, we still believe that there are a number of ways in which TwHistory could be enhanced. We believe this especially holds true if we consider other ways in which we could establish stronger adherence to the core principles of problem-based learning. In the following section, we will consider some of those possible enhancements, as that may aid readers and practitioners who wish to adopt or build on this framework.

TOWARD AN EVEN TIGHTER COUPLING
WITH PROBLEM-BASED LEARNING

As many readers of this volume are likely aware, problem-based learning originated in medical education as a response, in part, to problems that plagued medical instructors for years. Medical students were bored in large lecture-ormat basic science classes, they were unclear about what connection the coursework had to their future practice as doctors, and they struggled when they transitioned from passive learner to active participant in medical clerkships (Barrows, 1996). As a fundamentally pragmatic solution, Barrows simply started them in their clerkships from day one. Medical students were presented with patient cases and, in order to come up with meaningful diagnoses and treatment plans, the students had to acquire the relevant content knowledge associated with each patient case. Given only that background on PBL, it should be apparent that our intentions with TwHistory parallel those of Barrows. That is, we aimed to immerse students in an experience in which they are faced with an authentic task and must acquire relevant content knowledge associated with the specific situation at hand.

Yet, it is important to note that since its inception, PBL has become associated with many different definitions (Barrows, 1986, 1996), and it behooves us to be clear in this chapter about our own. Stated simply, we define PBL as an approach to education in which students are engaged in problems as a means to both acquire and apply knowledge. Furthermore, we understand PBL environments as containing the following characteristics:

- Problems are introduced first, before lecture, and the instructional experience is centered on the problems that are provided (Barrows, 1986).
- Problems are authentic. Each problem reflects situations that professionals might or currently do face. As part of that authenticity, problems are necessarily complex. They may cross over multiple disciplines and they are not constrained (Savery, 2006).
- Problems are ill-structured. It is not immediately apparent to students what they need to do in order to solve the problem. They first have to define the problem space, and there is enough room within that space to allow students to engage in free inquiry of surrounding issues (Barrows, 1986).

- Faculty act as facilitators. The instructors or tutors focus on guiding students, asking them meta-cognitive questions about their actions and problem solving process rather than correcting misunderstandings or providing information (Hmelo-Silver & Barrows, 2008).
- Students are at the center of a PBL experience. The students define learning issues that need to be pursued and take a leadership role with respect to their own education. Participants engage in self- and peer evaluation of their own efforts and the efforts of their group members (Barrows, 1996).
- Learning occurs in small groups. Typically, PBL happens in groups of 5–9 students. Groups divide up learning issues, individuals pursue them, and then results are shared with the group (Barrows, 1996).

PBL Alignment Challenges and Proposed Resolutions

TwHistory reenactments, like the Cuban Missile Crisis described above, share common ground with problem-based learning but could certainly be adapted better to the instructional approach. The following discussion elaborates on *PBL alignment challenges* with TwHistory alongside *proposed resolutions*. The high school students in Ms. F.'s class did pursue knowledge with a specific purpose in mind. However, their ultimate purpose was reproduction of a historical event. While reproduction is a task that a history enthusiast might engage in, its completion does not necessarily yield a resolution to an historical problem. Stated another way, the *PBL alignment challenge* is one of authenticity. TwHistory might be authentic relative to the work of history enthusiasts, but it may not be authentic relative to the work of *historians*.

A proposed resolution is to make TwHistory align closer to what historians do. To illustrate, consider what might happen with conflicts in primary source documents given the case of the Cuban Missile Crisis. White House/Khrushchev telephone transcripts could have conflicted with transcripts of Khrushchev's official radio addresses. While students may find these materials and conduct an ad hoc resolution of conflicting information, that process of resolving and reconciling the different primary sources is not the primary focus of their work. Their primary responsibility is to produce something that would make their virtual reenactment "work" when it is played out on Twitter. In effect, their primary goal was to "put on a show" rather than resolve a conflict in historical evidence.[5]

Were we to prioritize the historical reasoning processes of reconciliation and evaluation of source material (work more akin to what professional historians must do), the learning activity would need to be modified. One modification in this direction could have been made by prioritizing for the students the goal of reconciling conflicts in information sources. In that version, the students would have instead been advised, first and foremost, to pursue additional evidence about Khrushchev's motivations until they could make a well-justified historical argument.

An alternative resolution might be choosing a different form of professional practice. For example, in their social studies PBL effort, Saye & Brush (1999) asked students to advise President Truman on how to bring a speedy end to World War II. In that case, students faced the real problems and challenges associated with being a policy advisor. While not taking on the role of a historian directly, students would need to engage in similar research to make a meaningful recommendation. In the Cuban Missile Crisis, a comparable activity might have been to ask the students to behave as psychological profilers of Khrushchev and predict his reactions to various U.S. responses.

On the surface, TwHistory embodies the collaborative independent study featured in PBL. Learners engage in a divide-and-conquer approach where they research and investigate historical figures, then come together to share their knowledge, build a timeline, and prepare for the reenactment. However, the PBL alignment challenge is one of focus for each individual learner. Historical events are often retold with certain individuals playing more prominent or dominant roles. The addition of strong roles, and the identification of students with more prominent characters, represents another deviation from the core commitments of PBL. Canonical PBL activities involve students jointly collaborating on the same problem. Asking students to research and then play individual figures is more closely akin to other forms of inquiry, such as WebQuests (Dodge, 2001). In her responses to our questions, Ms. F. had reported to us that student groups in the Cuban Missile Crisis who had more prominent roles (e.g., John F. Kennedy) seemed more engaged in the learning experience. Some students, such as those with minor roles, were far less engaged in the reenactment process.

Rather than asking students to take on individual roles with varying amounts of importance, a proposed resolution is shifting research to a group responsibility. Having groups take on a collection of major as well as minor characters that are thematically related might facilitate more uniform engagement. For example, groups might be assigned all the historical figures from the United States, the Soviet Union, Cuba, or the United States Press. If the work were more evenly divided, we predict that engagement would be more evenly distributed. And if student groups were accountable to all aspects of the reenactment, we might expect that students would be even more likely to see important connections between and among pieces of historical evidence related to different individuals than when considering just one character.

Student engagement is certainly a feature of TwHistory, and students are at the center of their learning, but PBL alignment challenges persist. Specifically, TwHistory tends to lack in self- or peer evaluation and feedback.

For example, while Mrs. F. encouraged her Cold War History students to stay in character with their Twitter messages, they did not always do so. At one point in the reenactment, Khrushchev sent a message after conducting a nuclear test, and the students responsible for his character chose to have him tweet the anachronism, "Boo-yah!" A proposed resolution includes an increased emphasis on self- and/or peer-evaluation of effort. By sharing the burden of assuring all messages are in character and validating the historical authenticity of statements with students, teachers reinforce the idea that students play a central role in their learning process.

Our interview with Mrs. F. suggests she did well in acting as a facilitator rather than a traditional teacher. In particular, she noted that students were taking responsibility for their own learning. While not necessarily a PBL alignment challenge, here, facilitators can play a crucial role in either promoting or hindering student responsibility. Other research documents cases of facilitators lecturing to PBL groups when concerned that students were not learning enough (Moust, de Grave, & Gijselaers, 1990). Proposed resolutions for this kind of problem include a focus on meta-cognitive questioning and prompts (Hmelo-Silver & Barrows, 2008) as opposed to evaluative or corrective feedback. For example, in the case of the "Boo-yah!" message, the facilitator might ask a student or group of students to summarize the intent of the statement, to summarize what they know about Khrushchev, to review their profile of him and his speaking style, and then reconcile any inconsistencies they see. The facilitator might also ask students to support their tweets with primary source material. He or she would avoid labeling responses as correct or incorrect since it could undermine the learner-centered nature of the intervention.

Still more PBL-oriented adaptations could be made. Written scaffolds (e.g., McNeill, Lizotte, Krajcik, & Marx, 2006) that prompt students to engage in key steps of the PBL process could help. Such scaffolds might ask students to document their sources, and assigning credit to that documentation can help even further. Teachers may also choose to engage the class as a whole in the PBL activity, a choice with precedence (Barrows, Myers, Williams, & Moticka, 1986; Rangachari, 1996). While keeping to meta-cognitive questions, teachers may still need to be directive in terms of the PBL process, assuring students that they are on task and that the work is evenly divided. As a final proposed modification, TwHistory reenactments could be expanded to show off the process focus of PBL. Examining students' profiles of historical figures, their support for additions to the timeline, and explicit ties back to source documents would not only provide transparency for reenactment viewers, but it could peel back the curtain on how the work was done. Similar to Mrs. F.'s observation that her students started to think of primary documents as less scary, observers might be more willing to create their own TwHistory reenactments and more weight would be given to the process of creating the reenactment in addition to the product of the reenactment itself.

SUMMARY AND FUTURE WORK

The issues surrounding historical thinking and reasoning have drawn a great deal of attention in recent years, with greater attention being paid to the role that technology can play in this endeavor (e.g., Squire, 2003). This chapter presented one possible strategy for encouraging historical thinking through an integration of social media and problem-based learning. We offered a development and implementation framework in which we use the Twitter microblogging service as a platform for virtual historical reenactments. Specific examples were presented, including a re-enactment in a high school facilitated by a highly motivated and skilled history teacher. We are encouraged by the results of the Cuban Missile Crisis activity that this teacher led and believe that there is tremendous learning potential for virtual historical reenactments. In the past, Barrows questioned (2002) whether or not existing tools could support the processes of PBL at a distance. TwHistory may not be a direct response to this question since students worked in small face-to-face groups. However, TwHistory does provide an opportunity to show the products and perhaps the process of PBL learning in a way that is visible to a distance audience while simultaneously benefitting a local class.

More systematic design and evaluation work remains to be done. There are many potential spaces for improvement, particularly if we take seriously some of the features that have distinguished problem-based learning as an instructional method. Specific design variations might include changes in the types of problems presented, the nature of the group work, and the scaffolds provided to students to support peer review or focus their efforts. Given the dearth of existing research on social studies PBL environments, a great deal of investigation is needed about how these approaches impact student learning outcomes as well as more affective outcomes commonly associated with PBL such as motivation for learning, or satisfaction with the learning experience. The framework for reenactments in TwHistory presented here represents only a first step. We are encouraged about the prospects for work that transforms technologies emerging in the present into tools that help students delve into the past and ultimately could re-shape learning activities in the future.

NOTES

1. http://www.twhistory.org. TwHistory was conceived originally by Tom Caswell, Marion Jensen, and Rob Barton. The website provides free resources and guides for educators.

2. Notable instances of PBL implementations in the social sciences include Brush & Saye (2008); Gallagher, & Stepien (1996); Saye & Brush (1999).
3. http://www.socialoomph.com/
4. Responses were edited slightly for readability.
5. Similar conflicts are present in traditional media reenactments, which may be part historical project and part docudrama (Cook, 2004).

REFERENCES

Barrows, H. S. (1986). A taxonomy of problem-based learning methods. *Medical Education, 20*(6), 481–486.

Barrows, H. S. (1996). Problem-based learning in medicine and beyond: A brief overview. *New Directions for Teaching and Learning, 68,* 3–12.

Barrows, H. S. (2002). Is it truly possible to have such a thing as dPBL? *Distance Education, 23*(1), 119–122.

Barrows, H. S., Myers, A., Williams, R. G., & Moticka, E. J. (1986). Large group problem-based Learning: A possible solution for the '2 sigma problem'. *Medical Teacher, 8*(4), 325–331.

Bass, R., Rosenzweig, R., & Mason, G. (1999). Rewiring the history and social studies classroom: Needs, frameworks, dangers, and proposals. *Journal of Education, 181*(3), 41–62.

Brown, J. S., Collins, A., & Duguid, P. (1989). Situated cognition and the culture of learning. *Educational Researcher, 18,* 32–42.

Brush, T. & Saye, J. (2008). The effects of multimedia-supported problem-based inquiry on student engagement, empathy, and assumptions about history. *Interdisciplinary Journal of Problem-Based Learning, 2*(1), 21–56.

Cook, A. (2004). The use and abuse of historical reenactment: Thoughts on recent trends in public history. *Criticism, 46*(3), 487–496.

Davison, A., & Gordon, P. (1978). *Games and simulations in action.* London, UK: Woburn Press.

Dodge, B. (2001). Focus: Five rules for writing a great webquest. *Learning & Leading with Technology, 28*(8), 6–9, 58.

Ertmer, P. A., & Simons, K. D. (2006). Jumping the PBL implementation hurdle: Supporting the efforts of K–12 teachers. *The International Journal of Problem-based Learning, 1*(1), 40–54.

Gallagher, S., & Stepien, W. (1996). Content acquisition in problem-based learning: Depth versus breadth in American Studies. *Journal for the Education of the Gifted, 19*(3), 257–275.

Gijbels, D., Dochy, F., Van den Bossche, P., & Segers, M. (2005). Effects of problem-based learning: A meta-analysis from the angle of assessment. *Review of Educational Research, 75*(1), 27–61.

Hertel, J., & Millis, B. (2002). *Using simulations to promote learning in higher education.* Sterling VA: Stylus Publishing.

Hmelo-Silver, C. E., & Barrows, H. S. (2008). Facilitating collaborative knowledge building. *Cognition & Instruction, 26,* 48–94.

Hynd, C., Holschuh, J. P., & Hubbard, B. P. (2004). Thinking like a historian: College students' reading of multiple historical documents. *Journal of Literacy Research, 36*(2), 141–176.

Jenkins, H. (2009). *Confronting the challenges of participatory culture: Media education for the 21st century.* Cambridge, MA: The MIT Press.

Jones, K. (1987). *Simulations: A handbook for teachers and trainers.* London, UK: Kogan Page.

Lave, J., & Wenger, E. (1991). *Situated learning: Legitimate peripheral participation.* Cambridge, UK: Cambridge University Press.

Lenhart, A., & Madden, M. (2005). *Teen content creators and consumers.* Pew Internet & American Life Project. Retrieved from http://www.pewinternet.org/PPF/r/166/report_display.asp

McDaniel, K. N. (2000). Four elements of successful historical role-playing in the classroom. *The History Teacher, 33*(3), 357–362.

McNeill, K., Lizotte, D. J., Kracjik, J., & Marx, R. W. (2006). Supporting students' construction of scientific explanations by fading scaffolds in instructional materials. *Journal of the Learning Sciences, 15*(2), 153–191.

Moust, J. H., de Grave, W. S., & Gijselaers, W. H. (1990). The tutor role: A neglected variable in the implementation of problem-based learning. In Z. H. Nooman, H. G. Schmidt, & E. S. Ezzat (Eds.), *Innovation in medical education: An evaluation of its present status* (pp. 135–151). New York, NY: Springer.

Nardi, B., Schiano, D., Gumbrecht, M., & Swartz, L. (2004). Why we blog. *Communications of the ACM, 47*(12), 41–46.

National Center for History in the Schools. (1996). *National standards for history* (Basic ed.). Los Angeles, CA: National Center for History in the Schools, University of California, Los Angeles.

Nelson, L. M. (1999). Collaborative problem solving. In C. Reigeluth (Ed.), *Instructional-design theories and models: A new paradigm of instructional Theory* (pp. 241–267). Mahwah, NJ: Lawerence Erlbaum Associates.

Rangachari, P. K. (1996). Twenty-up: Problem-based learning with a large group. *New Directions for Teaching and Learning, 68*, 63–81.

Savery, J. R. (2006). Overview of problem-based learning: Definitions and distinctions. *The Interdisciplinary Journal of Problem-based Learning, 1*(1), 9–20.

Saye, J. W., & Brush, T. (1999). Student engagement with social issues in a multimedia-supported learning environment. *Theory and Research in Social Education, 27*(4), 472–504.

Shelton, B. E., & Wiley, D. A. (2007). *The design and use of simulation computer games in education.* Rotterdam, The Netherlands: Sense Publishers.

Spoehr, K., & Spoehr, L. (1994). Learning to think historically. *Educational Psychologist, 29*(2), 71.

Squire, K. (2003). *Replaying history: Learning world history through playing Civilization III.* Unpublished doctoral dissertation, Indiana University, Bloomington, IN.

Walker, A., & Leary, H. (2009). A problem based learning meta analysis: Differences across problem types, implementation types, disciplines, and assessment levels. *Interdisciplinary Journal of Problem Based Learning, 3*(1), 12–43.

Walker, A., & Shelton, B. E. (2008). Problem-based educational games: Connections, prescriptions, and assessment. *Journal of Interactive Learning Research,* *19*(4), 663–684.

Wiley, J., & Voss, J. F. (1996). The effects of "playing historian" on learning in history. *Applied Cognitive Psychology, 10*(7), 63–72.

Wineburg, S. (2001). *Historical thinking*. Philadelphia, PA: Temple University Press.

CHAPTER 3

REPOWERING READING AND WRITING
Energizing Content Area Curriculum with Online Social Media

Debra A. Pellegrino and Mary P. Mahaffey

Students in K–12 education can benefit significantly from structured collaborative use of online social media (OSM) to support learning objectives in reading and writing. Teachers in K–12 education, higher education professionals, and preservice teacher candidates need instructional strategies to coordinate OSM with problem-based learning. This chapter seeks to understand how directed use of online social media and problem-based learning enhances student learning outcomes. The authors of this chapter, siblings who teach at the primary and university levels, repowered their literacy learning strategies at both levels by critically examining focused approaches to problem-based learning instruction (PBL). The authors provide recommendations for OSM to the classroom teachers in K–12 as well as those studying to become teachers on the undergraduate and graduate levels.

INTRODUCTION

The authors of this chapter, siblings who teach at the primary and university levels, repowered their literacy learning strategies at both levels by

Designing Problem-Driven Instruction with Online Social Media, pages 41–63
Copyright © 2012 by Information Age Publishing
41

critically examining focused approaches to problem-based learning instruction (PBL). PBL is an extension of the constructivist approach to learning. Cheaney and Ingebritsen (2005) trace constructivism to the late 1980s, where students constructed learning through their individual interactions with their world. Using PBL has energized the authors' belief in the value of constructivism to aid their students' mastery of knowledge. Furthermore, current tools of online social media (OSM) have enhanced the range of individual learning opportunities significantly beyond those available to constructivists in the 1980s. In addition, online social media offer collaborative opportunities that allow teachers to design authentic learning experiences for both college students and young learners. By utilizing online discussion through Skype, the primary classroom teacher and the college professor enhanced both reading and writing instruction in the primary classroom curriculum as the university students tapped the dynamic potential of online social media to interact with primary school children. After discussing their concerns about reading and writing skills, not only on the primary school level but also on the collegiate level, the authors developed practical approaches to foster learning for both primary school children and university students.

To begin, the college professor analyzed the writing of freshman students in an Introduction to Early Childhood college class. After assessing her students' writing and providing targeted objectives for each university student, she arranged for these undergraduate students to work with the primary school students through email; her goal for the university students was for them to become better writers through communicating carefully by email with the primary school children. By reading the email from their college student partners, the first graders improved their reading comprehension and writing as they read their messages and wrote back to their college e-pals. In fact, as the university professor observed, the university students took more time with their writing as they crafted written messages to their primary school-aged partners, thus solving one of the intractable problems facing university educators of teachers-in-training. Convincing them that writing skills matter as does the audience to which they direct their writing, the college teacher demonstrated that problem-based learning and OSM empower the learners. Rather than directly "teaching" writing as a disparate and isolated discipline, the primary and college teachers used PBL to combine theoretical issues discussed in the college classroom with authentic work from the primary school students. Although the process described in this chapter focuses on the elementary classroom, the authors believe that the chapter can be applied to middle and secondary school-aged children as well. Imbedding the instructional goal within a meaningful person-to person interaction enhanced the teaching of the authors and the learning of their students.

The chapter is organized into sections, each of which includes a portion of the authors' diaries (weblog) used during their monthly approach to problem-based instruction via online social media. Shim and Guo (2009) analyzed the level of study and the perceived value of using a weblog in a three-phase study that examined college students' perception of weblogs used in class. Dearstyne (2005) defined weblog as "a hierarchy of text, images, and media objects, and data arranged chronologically, that can be viewed in an HTML browser" (p. 39). The authors believe that weblogging fostered their collaboration and sharing of instructional strategies to enhance PBL in their reading and writing curriculum. According to McLaren (2004), e-learning (viewed as a set of internet tools—e-mail, chat rooms, file sharing and video-streaming) facilitates PBL.

The results of the authors' work verified that classroom teachers who utilize creative problem solving and hands-on, computer-based lessons improve student knowledge and skills. Today's practitioners lack the innovation of sound strategies and online resource tools to improve students' comprehension skills. By combining knowledge of reading research with the modeling and demonstration of authentic classroom learning outcomes, problem-based instruction will improve reading and writing skills by utilizing online social media.

Theory into Practice

New technology has forced teachers to adapt and change their knowledge and skills to ensure that today's students are problem solvers. Almost half a century after the Cold War era and launching of the Russian spacecraft, Sputnik, Luke and Freebody (1999) suggested a need for a new literacy strategy that benefits young children in their science content area: Being a child, being an adolescent and, indeed becoming literate, have changed in some fundamental ways. The toolkit of basic skills that served many of us well in the 1950s is inadequate today.

The influence of technology and online social media (OSM) influences literacy acquisition in the United States, and it requires a reformulation of instructional approaches geared towards fostering literacy. Through problem-based learning (PBL), primary school children have access to a broader range of knowledge for communicating and for providing information in their classroom studies. As educators with over thirty years of service, we viewed the Internet not as a threat but as a tool for developing complex instructional strategies that encourage students to apply decision-making skills to their use of the Internet. In addition, the Internet also created new problems. Classroom teachers need to address the concerns of student safety on a daily basis if they are going to provide reading assignments on the web. This chapter demonstrates that it is possible for classroom teachers to apply developmental scaffolding that guides curricular decisions through

OSM. Scaffolding, which focuses on specific teaching strategies aimed to support learning when students are first introduced to a new subject, offers students the foundation from which to understand new information that will be introduced during the next lesson. It also offers instructors the chance to examine how certain program software provides opportunities for students to develop their own construct of resources to improve communication skills.

Given the age difference between the college students and the first graders, it is appropriate at this point to share a web site that aided both the college professor and the primary classroom teacher as they sought to acquire updated information for OSM to use with their students. The tip came from the author's daughter, a recent communications graduate and now an online copy editor. By visiting http://mashable.com/2011/01/07/online-education-websites/, educators and students can meet the changing curriculum of multiple literacies and keep current on skills, strategies, and practices through advances in technology. The chief goal of this partnership is to help students develop sound literacy practices from grades K–16. The university professor and classroom teacher employed OSM to assist their discussions of curriculum planning. Through the use of Skype, the college classroom connected university students to the students in the first grade classroom even though the schools were two hours apart.

The Energy from Vygotsky and Bruner

Russian psychologist Lev Vygotsky is not noted for coining the term *scaffolding*, yet by introducing educators to the term *zone of proximal development* (ZPD), Vygotsky (1978) showed that learners operate on two levels: the "actual developmental level" and the "potential developmental level." This distinction was essential to Bruner's later articulation of the concept of scaffolding. According to Vygotsky, "The ZPD is the distance between the actual developmental level as determined through problem solving under adult guidance or in collaboration with more capable peers" (p. 86).

Jerome Bruner (1976) defined a process "that enables a child or novice to solve a task or achieve a goal that would be beyond his unassisted efforts" (p. 90). Bruner applied the term, scaffold, to learning situations in reading and writing. By scaffolding, a reader improves comprehension when background knowledge is lacking.

As educators, the authors found that the process of scaffolding enhanced monthly lesson planning sessions in order to provide activities that supported and guided our learners, both university students and primary school students, to become proficient readers and writers. A Skype session was held twice a week between the university educator and the Classroom teacher. A blog recorded the daily notes of the two educators and helped them prepare for the Skype discussion. Table 3.1 compares the technol-

TABLE 3.1. Examples of OSM Tools and Instructional Strategies for the Academic Year

Monthly Category	Social Media/ Content Area	Instructional Strategy/Educational Use
September	*Skype/Blogs Science*	University and classroom teacher begin online reflections. Classrooms begin Skyping. Reading and writing skills become a priority in the science content area .Instructor posts lecture notes; students complete group homework; peer review of online reflections
October	*Skype/Wikis Social Studies*	Platform for group work where individuals in the group can collaborate on a project; edit and have a running commentary on the progress of the project
November	*Skype/Blogs Social Studies*	Instructors can use it for announcements and running dialogue with student questions; learners have the capability to provide comments on posts
December	*Skype, Claymation Reading*	Platform for online synchronous learning; Claymation was revisited to enhance sequencing, vocabulary development.
January– February	*SkypeiTunes/Science, Prezi, cell phones, flip video, Webmail*	Provides pre-lecture material, post-lecture replay to increase the depth of learning; tutorials or educational videos; interactive group presentation and feedback
March–May	*Skype/VoiceThread Claymation, Blabberize Email, Social Studies*	Recycling and retelling; platform for online synchronous learning; instructors can "meet" with students during virtual office hours

ogy used, the content areas covered and the curriculum-planning sequence throughout the school year. The university and primary school teachers, as well as the university students, utilized the blogger.com for their weblog discussions. According to Kirkpatrick and Droth (2005), the Blogger.com, owned by Google, is the largest blogging service available to the public for e-mail and instant messaging. The blogger.com site offered the instructors an accessible and economical opportunity to provide electronic journaling for their students.

CONVERSATIONS WITH WEBLOGGING

Vygotskian theories (Cole, 1996; Wertch, 1998) consider instructional tools as socially constructed signs. What happens when technology becomes a tool for literacy learning? As children interact with adults, peers, and technology, are they making meaning with the text? The authors related their own meaning making through online discussion beginning in early September of the academic year.

September

The socio-economic backgrounds of the university and primary school children were in alignment, as the majority of students on both levels came from financially sound homes. According to the primary school classroom teacher, these 17 children entered first grade with a love for books and a variety of skills from emergent literacy to fully proficient skills. Many first graders have been at the primary school since age three, and, since this institution is a private school, the majority of children experienced a home with a print-rich environment and access to the latest in technological gadgets.

The primary school children were introduced to an author study by their classroom teacher. Having the objectives of building community, scaffolding reading and writing skills, and using technology led the primary school classroom teacher to begin with a colorful, well-known author Eric Carle, a webblogger and author/illustrator over seventy picture books. In fact, during the late 1960s Carle began creating books for children and working with hand-painted tissue papers; he later embraced OSM. As the first graders increased their science observation skills using their classroom butterfly house, their literacy skills also improved as they read and reread the books by Eric Carle.

Primarily, the six-year old students were beyond the emergent literacy skills of understanding the skills of concept of word and alphabet recognition, which provided another reason for the classroom teacher to employ the Carle books. PBL connected the science curriculum with reading and writing skills. The students engaged in observation skills by recording data of what they saw, smelled, and heard. Children gathered milkweed plants and caterpillars from their own backyards. When the caterpillars were added to the butterfly house, the first graders started drawing diagrams of the caterpillars, cocoons and butterflies and writing their daily observations in their journals. After using the Smart Board in the primary school classroom to visualize graphic organizers, the first-grade students constructed their own graphic organizers following the categories of the five senses. PBL and OSM aided the students as they recorded their own observations into five categories (sight, sound, taste, touch, and smell). While the primary school teacher was building community with their peers, the university professor was introducing the term of a balanced literacy classroom to the university students.

The balanced literacy approach blends the two approaches of phonics and whole language to the classroom. The university students were being introduced to the importance of the read-aloud strategy when teaching the primary grades, and the classroom teacher was daily introducing the read-aloud activity to her students as a beneficial component to the content-area classroom.

The university students began researching children's literature by Eric Carle as the primary classroom teacher shared her lesson-planning with the university students and explained her decision of using the various books by Carle with bold, colorful illustrations. The university students used a web cam to view the first grade classroom and concluded that the display of fictional children's books with real-world artifacts of actual colorful butterflies was beneficial to building a positive working classroom community in the first-grade classroom. In the science classroom the young students were constructing learning from actual artifacts in their own environment to gain knowledge about insects. PBL and OSM had the students excited and engaged in learning and with each other. When the students listened to their teacher and peers providing oral readings of Eric Carle's *Very Hungry Caterpillar,* they synthesized the story by using technology and cartoon making. Reading comprehension improved for the first-graders as the primary students listened to the retellings of the Carle's text. The young readers created their story characters with clay animation so they could retell the story to each other by creating their own movie cartoon. The movie-making project certified that PBL was beneficial to literacy learning. In the movie world, clay animation has existed for at least fifty years, although creating movies for checking for reading comprehension was a new strategy for the classroom teacher.

Many classroom teachers have been reluctant to embrace the art of cartoon making or storyboarding, possibly because of their personal fears of technology. The university college students viewed cartoon making and OSM as a unique twist to their PBL strategies.

Resources for Future Educators

Resources on the web provided useful software packages for educators to purchase but are not required. The various steps in storyboarding for PBL are as follows:

1. Begin with a simple story plot for the first grade classroom. (Beginning-Middle and End) or (Characters/Setting-Problem/Conflict and Solution). For example, the butterfly—where does it begin? How does it grow? How does it transform? (The following websites offered added resources for step 1:Atomic Learning's FREE Video StoryBoard Pro Software for Mac and Windows http://www.atomiclearning.com/freestoryboard.shtml; Script writing and storyboard software (FREE) for Windows http://www.writingsource.com/software.html; Inspiration Software for Mac or Windows http://inspiration.com/)

2. Draw the stages of development of the life cycle of the butterfly

3. Roll out the clay and begin making the stages of the butterfly from clay
4. Create a lightweight sculpture out of pipe cleaners, Styrofoam, and aluminum foil
5. Wrap the sculpture with a "skin" of clay (Van Aken Claytoon clay works well— Retrieved from: http://www.vanaken.com/claytoon.htm)
6. Sculpt magnets into the feet for stability and place on a metal cookie tray. Use paper or images from the computer to depict the butterfly's environment, such as leaves, flowers, regions, and so on.
7. Take a break and read the *Very Hungry Caterpillar* by Eric Carle or other fiction or nonfiction literature on butterflies.

Figure 3.1 showcases the first-grade students as they began their journey with the University of Scranton students. The PBL approach through the daily Skype sessions enhanced meaningful learning outcomes for both groups of students. The primary school students used the various centers in the primary classroom to construct their own retelling of the story. The

FIGURE 3.1. The first grade students use Skype to connect with the Univeristy of Scranton students. Conversations between the two groups enhance content knowledge in science and social studies areas and reading and writing increases. (Permission given for photos by Mrs. M. Mahaffey's first grade parents at Harrisburg Academy, Womleysburg, PA. 2010)

webcam in the butterfly house assisted steps in the science implementation of content knowledge and observation skills as well as classroom management.

Skype and other tools of OSM presented university preservice teachers the opportunity to apply constructivist learning theory with the primary school students. The university students constructed their own decisions concerning classroom management strategies while promoting better relationships between themselves and their e-pals. The lack of focus on classroom management in university preservice instruction is the number one criticism of preservice teachers concerning their university professors. Clifford H. Edwards (2011) provided evidence in his book, *Democratic Discipline in Learning Communities*, of ways that schools fail to satisfy student needs and thus promote discipline problems. Teachers who pay special attention to children's need for self-direction can empower their students to become more intrinsically interested in school learning.

The first-grade students learned observation skills, science inquiry, and how to be patient while observing. Students value teacher relationships that make them feel worthwhile, support their independence, motivate them to achieve, and help them interpret and cope with environmental demands (Pianta, 1999).

The University students were indirectly using OSM to aid their PBL for curriculum development. An assignment for the university students included resourcing a variety of web sites to assist the primary classroom's curriculum planning. Both teachers benefitted from receiving the resources of web sites for content-area curriculum, and the university students were building their own portfolios for future references. Table 3.2 combines websites retrieved by the university students with observations provided by the classroom teachers during the curriculum development process.

Resources from Future Teachers
- How to Create Clay Animation in 5 Easy Steps—http://www.sfsu. edu/~teachers/workshops/clayanimation/index.html
- Tech4Learning Clay Animation Kit and Tutorials and Classroom Ideas—http://www.tech4learning.com/claykit/index.html
- The Clay Animation How to Page—http://www.animateclay.com/
- Clay Animation Station—http://library.thinkquest.org/22316/ home.html
- The Magic of Animation—http://ali.apple.com/ali_sites/ali/exhibits/1000678/Resources.html{\UNL}

During a Skype session in September, the university preservice teachers read excerpts from Donald Graves' (1989) book, *Investigate Nonfiction*.

TABLE 3.2. Resources for Future Teachers

OSM/ Web Sites	Observations of Educational Use
Software to use with a digital still camera Retrieved from: http://www.sfsu. edu/~teachers/workshops/clayanimation/ stepfive.html	After still pictures are taken for student projects, the pictures can be downsized and printed to create a flip book for each student.
Still cameras can be used to create animation in a flip-book. Emergent readers enjoy retelling and stay focused on the learning process for reading comprehension.	
Frame Thief (demo download) capture software to use with a webcam or a digital still camera Retrieved from: http://framethief.com/	Post-it notes were used by the students on each frame. Writing becomes part of the science lesson.
iStopMotion (demo download/shareware) capture software to use with a webcam Retrieved from:.http://www.istopmotion. com/	Writing development continues as students become engaged with character development.
Video Blender (Mac/Win) capture and editing software to use with a webcam, video, or digital still camera to capture the frames and edit the video Retrieved from: http://www.tech4learning. com/videoblender/index.html	"My wings are damp." exclaimed one student as they edited the video. No problems existed in classroom management as students were fully engaged in the learning process.
Stop Motion Animator (FREE!) capture software to use with a webcam Retrieved from: http://www.clayanimator. com/english/stop_motion_animator.html	Webcam videos offer a virtual view of each stage of development in the science classroom.
Digital still camera to capture the frames and edit the video Retrieved from: http://www.stopmotionpro. com/trial.htm	When each still is captured, action verbs become the focus with PBL.

Kaminski and Rezabek (2000) defined e-learning as a set of Internet tools (e-mail, chat rooms, video-streaming, threaded discussions, file sharing, etc.). The preservice teachers communicated with their peers via the university's software system, and students in online threaded discussion enhanced their comprehension of Graves' text by implanting the instructional goal within the personal interaction of threaded discussion. The preservice teachers focused on the realistic skills of reading and writing in order to attain deeper understanding of the content. Threaded discussions reinforced the concepts to the university students that learning provides the receiver the opportunity to listen and respond via OSM. So often, reading is not social, and being literate means reading and writing without the essential elements of speaking and listening. Online social media need to interweave reading, writing, speaking, and listening in order to provide opportunities for literate engagement.

As the discussion continued via the web, the college students began to take responsibility for their own learning. The university professor's scaffolding strategies worked, and this was assessed by reviewing the university students' lesson planning and online chats. The emails began to increase between college student and college student, students and teacher, and teacher and students. The sharing and growth with OSM reminded the university students about connecting the concepts and collaborations of literacy teaching. Frank Smith (1988) called this concept the "literacy club." When everyone has the expectations to learn and to do well including the teacher, who wants to master the skill of instructional delivery, the theory of joining the learning process became apparent. In the learning process, everyone thinks of themselves as members. This concept reflected the understanding of Smith's (1988) terminology of the "literacy club."

October

OSM was allowing the university professor and her university students and the classroom teacher and her primary school students to connect and to learn together through PBL. Teachers and students on many levels of learning connected writing skills through diaries, Skype, Facebook, and classroom projects. In fact, October's product of building the avatar sculpture became the month to build the university and primary school students' personal interactions through OSM.

After rereading the blog post, the university students noticed that science content knowledge was the trigger for the first-grade students to scaffold their reading and writing skills. In fact, just as one needs to reboot one's computer after shutting down, the future classroom teachers repowered their understanding of PBL. The month of October approached, and the classroom teacher concentrated on social studies content knowledge with the hope of providing meaningful person-to-person interactions between college students and the first graders.

The university students motivated the primary school students to write by using emails and Skype. At times, it was difficult for the primary school students to respond to the volume of emails, because the student-to-student interactions were met with such eagerness by the young students.

When the package from the university students arrived via snail mail for the first graders, the package was covered in dark blue paper with a variety of movable stick-on eyes decorating the paper. The package provided an illusion of a mystery box. In preparing the package, the college students utilized their best penmanship and wrote individual letters to their first-grade partners. The college students' letters included vocabulary that allowed the opportunity for the primary school students to utilize their environment and construct their own knowledge base by searching through dictionaries and nonfiction picture books already in the first-grade classroom.

Scaffolding vocabulary was a huge success, and the social studies concepts became easier to grasp for PBL by the primary school students. After receiving the letters from the college students, some first graders were frustrated because they knew that the vocabulary was challenging. The college students used adjectives and descriptive words that added deeper understanding and factual knowledge of the animals of the night. One letter described animals of the night as nocturnal. The students immediately wanted to know more about nocturnal animals and use this new vocabulary word in their own writing. This was a new realization for the first-grade students, bridging the visual understanding of what the theme of the package represented to the knowledge-based understanding of the word "nocturnal."

The university and primary school students' vocabulary learning was enhanced by a software program called Wordle®, a computer program for displaying words. Through PBL the preservice teachers began to understand that language has a function and students needed to use language in order to think, talk, and write about science concepts. OSM assisted the primary school students as they created Wordles for their university partners. The primary school students were having fun and increasing their content vocabulary as they tried to challenge their university e-pals. Quality children's literature and electronic e-pal letters supported authentic situations for primary school children and the university preservice teachers to problem solve and to generate their own questions about the content that they were learning in the classroom. Wordle acted as an educational toy for primary students to build their own vocabulary clouds, while at the same time it introduced a new instructional strategy for the university students.

The primary classroom teacher introduced creative projects in lesson planning for another layer of vocabulary development. The concept of creating an avatar was a novel idea for the university students to observe through webcam. As the classroom teacher utilized the internet site http://www.buildyourwildself.com (avatars), so did the university students. The university students used this OSM in order to instruct the first graders on how to use adjectives when describing a noun, such as an avatar. Many university students added this "Guess the Wordle" site (http://www.guessthewordle.pbworks.com) in their e-portfolio to reserve for later PBL use. The preservice teachers blogged about the inherent fundaments that Wordle created when describing avatars. The site, http://www.wordle.net/create, was identified as an OSM by the university students because they noticed that the primary school students became passionate about learning in an alternative way to traditional in-class instruction. They developed a deeper understanding for reading and writing when they were given an opportunity to learn in a social media context. Figure 3.2 shows the photo of the first graders on Skype with the university students.

Psychologist Vygotsky (1978) believed that through play, learners find their own zone of proximal development. The "zone" for a child is that region of performance in which the child can problem-solve only because of the presence and support: It is the distance between the actual developmental level as determined by independent problem solving and the level of potential development as determined through problem solving under adult guidance or in collaboration with more capable peers.

Literally, by playing with the computer software of Wordle, primary school age children created their own Wordles for their university student partners. The first graders created their Wordles through the use of their

FIGURE 3.2. This screenshot represents the beginning of a partnership between higher education and the K–12 school. The still picture was downloaded into a Smilebox® presentation for the university students to meet their new first grade e-pals. (Permission given for photos by Mrs. M. Mahaffey's first grade parents at Harrisburg Academy, Womleysburg, PA. 2010) (Permission given for photos by Mrs. M. Mahaffey's first grade parents at Harrisburg Academy, Womleysburg, PA. 2010)

imagination and problem-based learning, and designing an avatar for the college students empowered their experiences with content area learning. As Vygotsky points out, when children play, they create their own zone of proximal development.

On the university level, future teachers benefitted from observing their instructors relying on web-enhanced course instruction products. By receiving the Wordles from the first graders, new software instruction and OSM tools were introduced to the university students in a positive way. Researchers have investigated and reported that the overall success of e-learning initiatives, which include the collection of perceptual data from actual students, when paired with information technology in a classroom, justifies investment in information systems (Holsapple & Lee-Post, 2006).

November

The use of instructional technology and children's literature enhanced the weblogging during the month of November for the university students and primary school-age children. By examining the web-based diaries for November, the university students proceeded to use social studies content knowledge, technology, and writing skills in a broad-based way. Each web diary was arranged chronologically in the university students' free-style blogs. From the university students' perspectives, weblog usage added value to their curriculum development learning.

After researching a variety of theories (Callahan, Shim, & Oakley, 2000; DeLone, & McLEan, 2003; Dewey, 1938; Eisner, 1994; Freire, & Macedo, 1987; Hagood, 2000; Kessler, 2010) both authors agreed that the university students needed an authentic way to observe the variety of children's literature available for the primary classroom in the non-fiction and fictional genres. By using www.zoobooks.com or www.animal.discovery.com/guides/atoz/atoz.html plus the drawing program, Kid Pix®, the primary age students began to research bats while using PBL. Each student created his or her own presentation on one of the pages in *Stellaluna* by Janelle Cannon, a children's book about a mother and child bat. The university students downloaded the story of *Stellaluna* on their kindles or notebook computers. Through email, the university students asked the first graders to retell their stories in writing or in an artistic way. First, the stories were retold in a photo story, followed by the first graders' artistic creations by using Kid Pix (see Figure 3.3).

As the remaining months of the semester and school year continued, the university students continued reading the same children's literature that was present in the first-grade classroom and provided reading comprehension questions to the first-grade partners via email. The first graders answered the emails to their university partners with their own voice and a seemingly deeper understanding of context-based learning due to their

FIGURE 3.3.   First-grade students created the setting of Stellaluna using a Kid Pix program. Next, the image of the setting was downloaded into a photo story. (Permission given for photos by Mrs. M. Mahaffey's first grade parents at Harrisburg Academy, Womleysburg, PA. 2010)

own classroom experiences. Luke and Freebody (2000) define literacy as being a "flexible and sustainable mastery of a repertoire of practices with the texts of traditional and new communications technologies via spoken, print, and multimedia" (p. 9).

December

In December, the first graders completed their third author's study. After Carle and Cannon, this author's study focused on Jan Brett, a well-known children's author who concentrates on social studies content knowledge. Her fictional stories allowed literacy to develop to the fullest extent with the university and first grade students. Introducing an alternative genre in the classrooms allows new perspective into how a story is developed and communicated: the true embodiment of what literacy is.

The university students evaluated the first grade students mastering re-telling, sequencing of the story, and the importance of live text through speaking skills and drama. As the authors assessed the list of best practices in the university students' e-portfolios, the conclusion was to revisit Claymation as a new communication technology for literacy learning.

Claymation was revisited again in the first grade classroom. The process began by having the students view an online video with Jan Brett. The pre-service teachers visited www.janbrett.com. The first grade students watched the same video, "How to Draw a Baby Polar Bear" by Jan Brett. Together, the students learned how to draw a baby polar bear by watching the step-by-step video. Once the first grade students had a clear understanding of the size and texture of polar bears, each student made an animal research poster. The university students viewed this website: http://techtroj.pbworks.comn. The preservice teachers collaborated with their e-partners by researching polar bears. The first graders created a three-dimensional polar bear in its habitat (Figure 3.4). A polar bear image was taken by using a digital camera. Both the animal research and the image were imported into a *prezi®* by using the following website: http://www.prezi.com.

Through this website, the first grade students were able to demonstrate the volume of interesting facts by labeling parts of the polar bear picture and story-tell how polar bears live and move and adapt to their habitat. The first graders' presentations were sent live to their e-pals. PBL enabled the first graders to understand geographical regions and how the polar bears are structured for survival in these regions.

Reading researchers stated that a literacy program focused on developing multiliteracies would use the following understandings:

FIGURE 3.4. Flat image pictures were downloaded through the prezi software and revisited claymation to demonstrate polar bears in motion. (Permission given for photos by Mrs. M. Mahaffey's first grade parents at Harrisburg Academy, Womleysburg, PA. 2010)

- A text may be paper, electronic, or live.
- A text may compromise one or more semiotic systems.
- Texts are consciously constructed.
- Meanings are actively constructed.
- A text may have several possible meanings.

February

"What are shadows?" became the theme of the month of February. The university students and the first-grade students processed the inquiry method of shadows by constructing a game for the university students to guess a silhouette of their e-pals. The classroom teacher realized the Smart Board in her classroom could be used to demonstrate that when light is blocked, a shadow is formed. A flip video camera recorded each first grader's silhouette as he or she moved in front of the smart board projector. The silhouettes were downloaded in the Smilebox program and received by the e-pals in their webmail.

The university students Skyped their pen pals and assessed their educated guess of the silhouettes. In fact, the university students realized that PBL and OSM made the old-fashioned guessing game even more fun. When students have fun learning, classroom discipline decreases.

The university students decided to create their own shadow game by sharing their campus with their e-pals. The university students' flip cameras and cell phones became valuable instructional tools as they shot outside shadow pictures around their campus. The pictures; emailed to the first-grade students, started the guessing game with the outside environment.

The first-grade students were enthusiastic as they guessed various sculptures, buildings, and trees on campus. Questioning techniques were introduced by the classroom teachers. The first graders were allowed to ask 20 questions before the answers were given by their e-pals.

In today's world, a multiliterate person is a problem solver and a strategic thinker. The text that we access shapes our attitudes, values, and belief systems. As educators, we must use multimedia (texts constructed from different media such as a newspaper, movies, or television) and multimodal texts (those that draw on different modes, such as listening and speaking). The university and primary classrooms were experiencing PBL in multiliterate environments.

RESPONDING TO THE REMAINING
MONTHS OF THE SCHOOL YEAR

With three months remaining in the school year, the first grade students were able to recall facts, and retell a story. The university students assessed the classroom of their primary-school partners as a safe and secure learning atmosphere. The college professor provided many case studies for the university students to examine on classroom environments and literacy learning. The university students were assigned the work of researchers (Land, 2001; Lingard, Hayes, & Mills, 2003; Lingard, Hayes, Mills, & Christie, 2003) who examined multiliteracies pedagogy.

The university students reflected on their changing pedagogy as well as the literacy skills utilized in the first-grade classroom. As the school year was coming to a close, the month of March provided an opportunity for addressing higher-order thinking skills with a light-hearted design. Strategic thinking and problem-solving approaches challenged each first-grade student with creating his or her own leprechaun trap in March. As the first graders read about the impish character called a leprechaun, the Skype discussions focused on strategic problem-solving activities to prepare for March 17.

The first graders set their traps on March 16 to try to catch a leprechaun. The university students provided an online blabberize message to the first graders from their leprechaun. An example of a student's trap as well as the written message from the leprechaun that was imported into the blabberize by the university partners can be viewed in the picture (retrieved from http://www.teachweb2.wikispaces.com/blabberize).

By April and May, the classroom focused on social and cultural diversity. Williams (2004) states that graphic organizers are effective visual prompts that support memory. Through the utilization of graphic organizers as a story map, young readers increased their story comprehension by having a visual tool to facilitate opportunities for critical discussions. Story maps dedicated to the organization of story and events became a tool for strategic thinking. In fact, graphic organizers helped the primary school readers remember and discuss characters in routine ways. OSM graphic organizers provided strategies for student and teacher interactions through routines on a daily basis.

In April, a creative arts project using the owl as a symbolic tool for knowledge of recycling enhanced the writing skills for the primary school children (Figure 3.5). The month of April in the first-grade classroom introduced primary students to the concept of sustaining one's resources. Recycled materials were used by both university and primary school students. Owls were created from recycled materials. After observing the first graders in art class via Skype, the university students introduced digital stories to their e-pal friends. The university students reviewed the art projects on the photos posted to the first graders' website and assessed their work by a rubric given by their professor. By using OSM with PBL, the university students who feel inadequate regarding their art knowledge inadvertently learned from the first-grade partners.

FIGURE 3.5. (Permission given for photos by Mrs. M. Mahaffey's first grade parents at Harrisburg Academy, Womleysburg, PA. 2010)

As Elliot Eisner (1988) concluded more than 20 years ago with his scholarly research, teachers do what they know how to do. In fact, if teachers' early art education was limited, then this limited perspective will continue until teachers are convinced that better alternatives are available. PBL with the tools in OSM provided increased alternatives for the university students to enrich their experiences in curriculum design with a creative process.

The authors of this chapter support the decision to incorporate PBL with OSM to university teacher education students in an authentic way by partnering with the K–12 classroom teachers. Approximately 75% of colleges and universities require only one course in the visual arts for preservice teachers, and others require none (Jeffers, 1993). The university students in this chapter were not required to take one course that covers in OSM or in the visual arts. The authors concluded unless preservice teachers are exposed to this preparation, the beginning teacher will hardly feel confident.

The experiences of the university students with their primary school partners provided an opportunity to work with a variety of literacy opportunities and online social media. By the time the first graders were ready to be promoted to second grade, their science and social studies content knowledge had improved and they had gained confidence in their own abilities to create and improve their reading and writing skills.

The first graders sent owl announcements electronically to their university student partners. After viewing the digital stories from their university partners, the first graders created their own digital stories. The university students discovered that the first graders understood the social science concept that owls are important predators that keep the ecosystems in balance. The first-grade students studied owls from tufts to talons, and they learned fascinating facts about many different species of owls found in the United States and Canada.

After the first graders created owls from recycled materials, their classroom teacher connected the math curriculum with their art project. The primary school students measured the owls in height and weight and made birth certificates to show the centimeters of each owl and their weight in grams. Graphs were created online to show the different sizes of each species of owl (Figure 3.5). Lesson planning and higher-order problem-solving strategies benefitted students in higher education as well as the first graders for a more literate community.

After repowering their learning with digital stories, the university students set the objectives to ensure their independent learning over the summer months with their primary school partners. During the month of May, the university students shared this website in their lesson planning: http://www.bighugelabs.com. Primary school children created their own trading cards to make facts about themselves and then mailed the cards to their university partners. The future teachers connected the idea of trading cards with the content areas, such as state cards for geography, authors for literature, fish identification cards for science or interesting places to visit for social studies, and so on. By focusing on themselves, they can then share their own dreams and imaginations.

CONCLUSION

After reflecting on the events of the academic year, the authors believe that the university students and primary students benefitted from taking small steps towards problem based learning. The OSM tools positively impacted students' and teachers' literacy learning. The poet William Stafford stated that it is these details in life that are the "golden threads" that lead us to "amazing riches." Stafford's poem "Things I Learned Last Week" (1982) summarizes the research of the authors that independent learners need to think for themselves, and to make decisions about their own learning both on the university or K–12 levels.

REFERENCES

Bruner, J. (2006). *In search of pedagogy: The selected works of Jerome S. Bruner.* London, New York: Routledge.

Callahan, E. R., Shim, J. P., & Oakley, G. W. (2000). Learning, information, and performance support (LIPIS): A multimedia-aided approach. *Interfaces, 30*(2), 29–40.

Cheaney & Ingebritsen. (2005). Problem-based learning in an online course: A case study," *International Review of Research in Open and Distance Learning.* [Accessed 2 March, 2006 from http://www.irrodl.org/content/v6.3/cheaney-ingebritsen.html].

Cole, M. (1996). *Cultural psychology: A once and future discipline.* Cambridge,MA: The Bellcup Press/Harvard University.

Cope, B., & Kalantzis, M. (2003). *Learning by design.* Altona,Victoria,Australia: Common Ground Publishing.

Dearstyne, B.W.(2005). Blogs, the new information revolution? *Information Management Journal, 39*(5), 38–44.

DeLone, W. H., & McLean, E. R. (2003). The DeLone and McLean model of information systems success: A ten year update. *Journal of Management Information Systems, 19*(4), 9–30.

Dewey, J. (1938). *Experience and education.* New York, NY: Touchstone.

Edwards, C. (2011). *Democratic discipline in learning communities.* New York, NY: Rowman & Littlefield.

Eisner, E. (1988). *The role of discipline art education in America's schools.* Los Angeles, CA: Center for Education in the Arts.

Eisner, E. (1994). *Cognition and curriculum reconsidered* (2nd ed.). New York, NY: Teachers College Press.

Freebody, P., & Ludwig A. (1990). Literacies programmes. Debates and demand in cultural contexts. *Prospect: A Journal of Australian TESOL* 00-20007, *5*(3), 1–18.

Freire, P., & Macedo, D. (1987). *Literacy: Reading the word & the world.* Westport, CT: Bergin & Garvey.

Graves, D. (1989). *The reading/writing teacher's companion: Experiment with fiction.* Portsmouth, NH: Heinemann Educational Books.

Hagood, M. (2000). New times, new millennium, new literacies. *Reading Research and Instruction, 39*, 311–328

Holsapple, C.W., & Lee-Post, A. (2006). Defining, assessing, and promoting e-learning success: An information systems perspective. *Decisions Sciences Journal of Innovative Education, 4*(1), 67–85.

Jeffers, C. (1993). A survey of instructors of art methods classes for preservice elementary teachers. *Studies in Art Education, 34*(4), 233–243.

Kaminski, K., & Rezabek, L. (2000). *Student perceptions: Printing activities' influence on satisfaction with web-based instruction.* Paper presented at the National Convention of the Association for Educational Communications and Technology, Denver, CO.

Kessler, S. (2010). *Seven fantastic free social media tools for teachers.* Mashable. Retrieved from http://mashable.com/2010/10/16/free-social-media-tools-for-teachers/

Land, R. (2001). *The Queensland school reform longitudinal study. Teachers' summary.* Brisbane, Australia: The State of Queensland Educational Department.

Lingard, B., Hayes, D., & Mills, M. (2003). Teachers and productive pedagogies: Contextualizing, conceptualizing, utilizing. *Pedagogy, Culture and Society. 11*(3), 399–424.

Lingard, B., Hayes, D., Mills, M., & Christie, P. (2003). *Leading learning: Making hope practical in schools.* Buckingham, UK: Open University Press.

Luke, A. & Freebody, P. (2000, August). Further notes on the four resources model. *Reading Online, 3.* Available: http://www.readingonline.org/past/ past_index.asp?HREF=/research/lukefreebody.html.

Luke, A., Freebody, P., & Land, R. (2000). *Literate futures: Review of literacy education. Brisbane.* Qld: Education Queensland.

McLaren, C.H. (2004). A comparison of student persistence and performance in online classroom business statistics experiences. *Decision Sciences Journal of Innovative Education, 2*(1), 1–10.

Pianta, R.C. (1999). *Enhanced relationships between children and teachers.* Washington, DC: American Psychological Association.

Roblyer, M. D. (2002). Educational technology in context: The big picture. In M.D. Roblyer (Ed.), *Integrating educational technology into teaching* (ch. 1). Upper Saddle River, NJ: Prentice Hall.

Shim J. P., & Guo, C. (2009). Weblog technology for instruction, learning, and information delivery. *Decision Sciences Journal of Innovative Education, 7*(1), 171–193.

Smith, F. (1988). *What the brain does well.* Victoria, B.C.: Abel Press.

Stafford, W. (1982). Things I learned last week. In *Glass Face in the Rain* (p. 66). Portland, OR: Estate of William Stafford.

Vygotsky, L. S. (1978). *Mind in society. The development of higher psychological processes.* Cambridge. MA: Harvard University Press.

Wertch, J. V. (1991). *Voices of the mind: A Sociohistorical Approach to Mediated Action.* Cambridge: Harvard University Press.

Williams,N. (2004) *Using literature to support skills and critical discussions for struggling readers: Grades 3–9.* Lanham, Md.: Scarecrow Education.

Wood, D., Bruner, J.S., & Ross, G. (1976). The role of tutoring in problem solving. *Journal of Child Psychology and Psychiatry, 17*(2), 89–100. Doi:10.111/j.1469-7610.1976.tb00381.x (n.d.).

Children's Literature

Brett, J. (2005). *Three snow bears.* New York. NY: G. P. Putnam's Sons.

Cannon, J. (2007). *Stellaluna.* New York, NY: Houghton Mifflin.

Carle, E. (1994). *The Very Hungry Caterpillar.* New York, NY: Penguin Group.

Technological Resources:

Retrieved from: http://www.sfsu.edu/~teachers/workshops/clayanimation/step-five.html.

Still cameras can be used to create animation in a flip book. Emergent readers enjoy retelling and stay focused on the learning process for reading comprehension. After still pictures are taken for student projects, the pictures can be downsized and printed to create a flip book for each student.

Frame Thief (demo download) capture software to use with a webcam or a digital still camera. Retrieved from: http://framethief.com/ Post-it notes were used by the students on each frame. Writing becomes part of the science lesson.

iStopMotion (demo download/shareware) capture software to use with a webcam Retrieved from: http://www.istopmotion.com/ Writing development continues as students become engaged with character development.

Video Blender (Mac/Win) capture and editing software to use with a webcam, video, or digital still camera to capture the frames and edit the video Retrieved from: http://www.tech4learning.com/videoblender/index.html "My wings are damp," exclaimed one student as they edited the video. No problems existed in classroom management as students were fully engaged in the learning process.

Stop Motion Animator (FREE!) capture software to use with a webcam Retrieved from: http://www.clayanimator.com/english/stop_motion_animator.html.

Webcam videos offer a virtual view of each stage of development in the science classroom. Digital still camera to capture the frames and edit the video. Retrieved from: http://www.stopmotionpro.com/trial.htm When each still is captured, action verbs become the focus with PBL

UNIT 3

HIGHER EDUCATION

CHAPTER 4

A DESIGN MODEL OF HARNESSING WIKI FOR COLLABORATIVE PROBLEM-BASED INSTRUCTION IN HIGHER EDUCATION

Ying Xie and Seung Kim

Based upon a thorough review of current literature that empirically employed wiki for students' collaborative problem-based instruction (PBI) in higher education classrooms, this chapter identifies key design considerations for how to harness this popular Web 2.0 tool to promote learning and collaboration in PBI. We describe and analyze selected cases, noting especially the interrelationship of learning objectives, problem choices, pedagogical practices and implications for designing wiki-supported PBI. To conclude, this chapter proposes a model, namely "P3A," representing "Preparation, Pedagogy, Participation and Assessment," to illustrate the design process of incorporating wiki for collaborative PBI. We make recommendations for instructional practices to facilitate problem-based learning with Web 2.0 tools.

Designing Problem-Driven Instruction with Online Social Media, pages 67–86

INTRODUCTION

Problem-based instruction (PBI) is an educational practice in which students, usually working in teams, actively resolve complex problems in realistic situations (Savin-Baden & Major, 2004). In recent years, higher education has seen an increasing emphasis on providing opportunities for students to enhance problem-solving and critical-thinking skills through working and collaborating in groups. In addition, the paradigm for higher education has shifted from lecture-based instruction to active and constructive learning due to a greater institutional focus on the quality of students' learning experiences. This shift has also placed pronounced emphasis on the use of instructional technology to promote various learning processes including PBI (Barr & Tagg, 1995). Wiki, a Hawaiian word meaning quick, in particular, separates itself from other emerging technologies with its many unique features including collaborative and asynchronous authoring of contents, easy display of editing history, and so on. Despite the fact that wiki has been increasingly used for collaborative problem-solving as indicated by the literature, it is still not clear how wiki has been employed to facilitate problem-based instruction in higher education and what the design implications are from these implementations. The purpose of this chapter is to review the studies that engaged students in wiki-supported PBI, to examine the design considerations of using wiki for PBI, and to suggest effective instructional strategies for the design and implementation of PBI using this collaborative technology tool.

BACKGROUND

Collaborative Problem-Based Instruction

Problem-based instruction refers to a strategy that confronts students with conceptually ill-structured problems and engages them in the activity of reaching meaningful solutions (Rhem, 1998). Boud and Feletti (1997) advocate that a PBI activity should encourage students to work with their peers in groups on finding solutions to a number of complex problem sets in real-world scenarios. In a team environment, students are encouraged to build skills related to collective decision making through dialogue and negotiation, conflict resolution, and team leadership. Major characteristics of collaborative PBI usually include:

- authentic problems as the driving force in tutor-led groups, with potentially multiple outcomes
- effective use of an integrated, flexible, and usable knowledge base
- continuous monitoring and assessment of the adequacy of their knowledge problem solving and self-directed learning skills
- effective collaboration as a member of a group

- emphasis on performance-based assessments. (Savin-Baden & Major, 2004)

Esch (2000) distinguishes problem-based learning from project-based learning by the trigger of the task and the learning model each activity involves. Project-based learning typically starts with an end-product of an *artifact* in mind, whereas in problem-based learning, the trigger is often an ill-structured problem reflecting real-life cases. In terms of the learning model, project-based learning uses a production model, while problem-based learning employs an inquiry model. The focus of this chapter is about *problem*-based instruction processes using wiki instead of *project*-based instruction.

According to Uden and Beaumont (2006), in collaborative problem-based instructional design, the following factors are important: the domain, the structure of the curriculum, the problem trigger, grouping of teams, the tutor's roles, and the assessment of the PBI activities. Research has shown that students could benefit from PBI in many ways: for example, (1) increased interest and engagement of students (Barrows & Tamblyn, 1986), (2) improved interpersonal and communication skills (Engel, 1997), (3) escalated transferrable skills (Woods, 1996), and so on. Nevertheless, some reports about restraints of this strategy showed that some students felt overwhelmed or overloaded (Ryan, 1997), and the success of PBI largely depended on students' access to resources (Heycox & Bolzan, 1997). With an increased emphasis on problem-solving and critical-thinking skills in higher education, instructors started introducing emerging technologies in an effort to create active learning environments to support group problem-solving processes. We now discuss the role Web 2.0, and wiki in particular, could play in a collaborative PBI activity.

PBI with Wiki

According to Barr and Tagg (1995), active learning environments should lead students to discover and construct knowledge for themselves. Web 2.0 could play an important role in creating such a learning environment. Web 2.0 refers to a trend of World Wide Web technologies encouraging creative and constructive information-sharing and communication. Such technologies include weblogs (online journal systems, e.g., blogger. com), wikis (collaborative websites editable by a community of users, e.g., Wikipedia.com), video-sharing sites (e.g., youtube.com), social-networking sites (e.g., facebook.com), and so on. The constructive and sharing nature of such technologies offer a number of educational advantages and pedagogical benefits. For example, wiki, one of the popular Web 2.0 technologies, is identified as a major learning technology that can be used to engage students in interactive activities (Baird & Fisher, 2005). Most wikis share some common features, including multi-user editing, link embedding, editing history display, and search functions within the wiki pages (Ebersbach, Glaser, & Heigl, 2006). Andrew (2008) suggests that with these features, wiki technology makes it easy to work on a collaborative project, track work progress, and manifest each individual's contribution.

Wikis have been introduced into colleges and universities and explored as a teaching tool (Konieczny, 2007). Some assignments and activities suited for a wiki may include brainstorming sessions, group discussions, knowledge-base creating, and collaborative writing (Hsu, 2007). Besides offering a space for students to co-construct knowledge in a socially negotiated environment (Nicol, Littlejohn, & Grierson, 2005), wikis can also be used in problem-based learning situations since. In essence, wiki is a user-directed discourse. When a group of students contribute to one discourse to reach a problem solution in PBI, students need to intensively interact with one another in order to find the communal response to the problem by way of dialogue and meaning-negotiation. To this end, shared understanding of experience and learning are greatly encouraged.

In order to find out how wiki has been used in collaborative PBI in higher education, we performed a complete review of the literature. Among a great number of empirical studies on wiki for students' collaborative learning, many of them mainly used wiki for collaborative *project*-based instruction; only a few studies used wiki for problem-based instruction in higher education. The following sections present summaries of some exemplary cases and identify a number of instructional design factors and recommendations for employing wiki for collaborative problem-based instruction.

EXAMPLES OF PBI WITH WIKI

Five cases are summarized in this section. The first three cases (Hazari, North, & Moreland, 2009; Robertson, 2008; Zorko, 2009) examined students' experiences and their perceived value of wiki for problem-based learning. The other two cases (Neumann & Hood, 2009; Williams, Woodward, Symons, & Davies, 2010) investigated the effect of using wiki-supplemented PBI on students' learning outcomes and engagement in the learning activities. Please note, in this review section of the chapter, we sometimes will use PBL (problem-based learning) to replace PBI to be consistent to the reviewed studies.

Case 1: Students' Experiences of Using Wiki for PBI

Robertson (2008) engaged vocational teachers in a collaborative problem-based learning activity in a blended learning approach (wiki supplementing face-to-face contact) in a teacher education course lasting for 13 weeks. During the first eight weeks, the instructor used lectures and tutorials to expose students to theories and models of workplace learning. Then students wrote individual papers (accounting for 60% of the total grade) as an assessment of learning during the first eight weeks. During the last five weeks, students were split into groups of four to five members, and each group was to develop a staff training plan for a given scenario on a wiki site. This assignment contributed to 40% of the total grade for the course.

Before the assignment, the instructor demonstrated how to use the wiki site and made suggestions about group collaboration including group dynamics, roles, and processes. To assist problem solving of the presented cases, the instructor directed students to consider and identify further information and met with each group face to face every week. Every group started with the same pre-prepared wiki template designed to scaffold the development of the training plan. The template included a home page, team details, design models and principles, considerations for the training plan, recommendations, records of meetings, references and resources. In addition, student groups were encouraged to customize the template to their own needs and liking. Upon completion, each group received a group grade for the training plan on the basis of presentation and content. Peer assessment was also conducted, with each group member rating his or her own and other group members' contributions to the final work. Individual grades were then assigned based on the group mark and peer evaluation. A post-course survey on the learners' experiences of access to and the use of wikis was handed out to the students. The majority of the students found wiki easy and flexible to use. Most students voted for flexibility as the best feature of wiki, which provided them access and use of the software at the same time from various locations. Other favorable features identified included the ability to track previous edits and submit and present their final work with the software. The teacher candidates indicated that wikis could potentially be used in their own teaching and would continue and maybe expand the use of wiki in their program.

In general, students had a positive experience using wiki to support their asynchronous collaboration on this problem-based project. In order to ensure the success of the problem-solving activity, the instructor embedded elements on the wiki to scaffold the problem-solving process. In addition, students also had many face-to-face meetings and garnered sufficient support from the instructor from the scheduled weekly meetings. Another factor that could have contributed to the success of the case might have been the peer assessment, which might have motivated all group members to participate in the activity.

Case 2: Factors Affecting Students' Collaborative PBI with Wiki

What are students' perceived factors that could either *encourage* or *hinder* their collaborative problem-based learning in the wiki environment?

In an "English for Specific Purposes" course for second-year sociology students, Zorko (2009) introduced wiki for students to work in small groups to solve an open-ended, real-life sociology problem. About 40 students were grouped into ten cohorts for this activity. Similar to Case 1, the wiki started with templates that served to scaffold the students' problem solving but allowed for their personalization. The sidebar of each cohort's wiki contained links to resources including guidelines for report writing. The cohorts were then instructed to conduct research, hold meetings, submit meeting minutes, write the research reports, and present them in class.

Overall, the results showed that wiki enhanced collaboration of students' language learning since many collaborative behaviors among students seemed to be promoted, including learning from each other and communicating with the teacher. Yet, students preferred using Instant Messenger and email to communicate with peers and co-construct products instead of wiki, mainly because the students had the opportunity to collaborate in live meetings. Students identified the following factors to have enhanced collaboration in the wiki: the visibility of everyone's work, the teacher's prompt response and encouragement, direct accessibility of resources and scaffolding on the wiki, user friendliness of the wiki site, and inclusion of students' contribution toward their final grade of the course. Nevertheless, the following factors seemed to have discouraged collaboration in the wiki: frequent face-to-face meetings (with such meetings, students do not feel the need to use wiki); preference for Instant Messenger, email, and mobile phone communication; technical glitches of the wiki site; and preference for publishing only the finished product on wiki (because of the public nature, students were hesitant to show their "messier" work in progress).

In addition to students' perceptions about wiki, the instructor felt that using wiki to supplement PBL substantially improved several problematical issues that had existed prior to introduction of the wiki. First, the wiki allowed the instructor to provide students with immediate feedback on their progress, whereas prior to having wiki, the instructor had no means of communicating such information to students promptly. Second, no longer limited by time and location constraints, most students were able to fully participate in group learning with easier communication within the group with the help of wiki. Also, knowledge sharing among students was greatly enhanced. Third, the visibility and traceability of student work on the wiki served as an impetus for all group members to equally participate in the creation of quality products. Without wiki, neither group members nor the instructor could track or evaluate an individual student's contribution to the group project. The design and findings of this case were very similar to Case 1, in that both used wikis to provide scaffolds and recourses, and students held face-to-face sessions to work collaboratively in both cases. The unique pedagogical design of this case was that the instructor used wiki to provide immediate feedback, which in turn greatly promoted students' motivation.

Case 3: Students' Perceived Pedagogical Value of Wiki for PBI

Compared to the first two cases, Hazari et al. (2009) took one step further to determine if factors such as age, gender, work experience, and web development experience could influence students' pedagogical value of wiki (PVW). In this case, the assignments selected for wiki-supported PBI included journal article critiques and a management consultant case report (case analysis and online presentation). To take advantage of the collaborative aspect of the technology, students were put into groups to complete this assignment. Students were given explicit requirements to assign roles and responsibilities within each group, set up protocols for interaction, establish deadlines, and proofread results before submission.

The case showed many variations in students' perceived PVW. In general, those students with more than five years' work experience perceived wiki to have less pedagogical value in comparison to students with no full-time work experience. Males valued wiki more than females, and younger students perceived wiki to have higher instructional potential than older students. These results seemed to indicate that students with different characteristics could probably have adopted this technology differently. Therefore, in future design, instructors should consider alternatives or provide more training and incentives for busier and less technology-savvy individuals, who might be unfamiliar with technology.

The students found that the wiki tool brought in a new approach for completing this PBI assignment, encouraged leadership in group activities, demonstrated group members' thinking processes, and prevented procrastinating. Yet some students expressed that it was hard to communicate and coordinate solely by using wiki, suggesting that wiki as the communication channel alone might not be enough for group communication during such collaborative problem-solving processes.

Case 4: Integration of PBL into Course Curriculum Helped Retention

In a recent study, Williams et al. (2010) restructured the whole curriculum by introducing the PBL (problem-based learning) component into the introductory inorganic/physical chemistry course. The modified course comprised 20 lectures, three workshops, and 18 one-hour PBL sessions. Lectures and workshops delivered learning content. One of the lectures introduced the PBL method and basic guidance on how to use the virtual learning environment with wiki. During the PBL sessions, 17 student groups, each with five to six members, met and worked on real-world scenarios on topics related to the preceding lectures.

In order to help students solve the problems, facilitators, after being trained, were available for assistance during PBL sessions. In addition, students received instructions about a series of necessary steps for tackling the problems, called SET:

S—Summarize the problem
E—Existing knowledge related to the problem
T—Things to find out to solve the problem (Williams et al., 2010, p. 35)

The course instructor and other facilitators created group wikis to deliver and update all groups with the problems, course announcements, PBL guidance and other resources, such as web links, podcasts, pdf study guides, and lecture notes. Each group could only access its own wiki. Besides creating wiki sites and providing PBL support, the instructor also offered suggestions for group dynamics, requiring all group members to define the problems and work collaboratively in planning, researching, and constructing solutions to the problem on a group wiki. Facilitators used the commenting feature to provide the groups with feedback, specifying the desired level of deliverables. Besides the wiki, each group had access to basic communication tools including a group forum, a group email function, and a file-sharing tool for coordinating its off-campus collaboration. Similar to Cases 1 and 2, peer assessment was carried out in this study in order to ensure a fair distribution of marks within each group.

At the end of the course, the instructor compared exam results of the current year's students with previous years when PBL was not a part of the curriculum. Student performance with PBL was similar, yet retention rate after the introduction of PBL had risen sharply (no student dropped the course with PBL). Participants' feedback showed that students seemed to have increased their transferable skills in the content area and improved on group collaboration, which could have led to high student retention within the PBL cohort.

This case was unique from previous cases in two ways. First, wiki-supported problem-based instruction sessions interwove with lectures throughout the semester, and each PBL session focused on one individual problem related to the previous lecture. In comparison, PBI activities appeared to be one short activity with varying lengths of duration in the first three cases. After a few sessions in this case, students had already adapted to the rhythm of the course and become familiar with the wiki technology. Second, the study meticulously carried out staff training for the facilitators on how to run the PBL sessions to prevent them from leading the discussions or over-specifying the responses. For a non-traditional instructional technique like PBL, facilitator training seemed to be essential for the success of such technique (Raine & Symons, 2005).

Case 5: Improved Student Engagement with Wiki in PBI

Neumann and Hood (2009) conducted a comparative study to measure the effect of using wiki for a PBI activity on learning outcomes, knowledge of report writing, attitudes towards statistics, statistics anxiety, and engagement with other students. In a first-year university statistics class, 52 students were introduced to statistics theory and application in psychological research and practice. During the first six face-to-face tutorial classes, students learned data analysis and report writing skills, including database searches for literature, statistical tests, and how to write the reports.

Then students were assigned into two conditions: with and without the use of wiki for report-writing. Students in the non-wiki condition analyzed a data set and wrote the report individually. In the wiki condition, students formed subgroups of four to six members, analyzed the same data, but jointly wrote a report on a wiki. The facilitator set up each subgroup's wiki, which was a component of the Blackboard learning management system, and restricted access to the facilitators and belonging subgroup members for each wiki. During a 15-minute introduction, the facilitator showed students how to access the wiki, edit information, add comments and contact for help. In addition, student groups could contact the facilitator during his/her consultation sessions for additional support in using the wiki. As each class moved from one specific content area to the next topic in a progressive manner, the facilitators kept adding more sections to the wiki accordingly while checking on the progress of each subgroup and answering technical questions.

Although there was no significant difference in students' performance between the wiki and non-wiki groups, student engagement was enhanced with the wiki. The results demonstrated that students in the wiki group had higher scores in the National Survey of Student Engagement, which is used to evaluate student social development, cognitive engagement, and skill development, and better class attendance than those who developed the report individually. The researchers concluded that wikis improved student collaboration and promoted their cognitive and intellectual learning processes. Cases 4 and 5 both suggested that students who were engaged in wiki-supported problem-based instruction were better involved in the learning activity socially and cognitively than those who were not using wiki or PBI.

In summary, the five cases using wiki for PBI in higher education showed certain successful results on students' learning perception, attitudes, and engagement with the course and group activity. In order to support effective PBI with wiki tools, instructors typically provide templates, resources, guidelines, and immediate feedback; set up protocols for interactions; establish deadlines; and assign roles or responsibilities. In the following section, we discuss practical guidelines in greater depth for planning wiki-supported collaborative PBI with a design model to ensure effective learning.

INSTRUCTIONAL STRATEGIES FOR PBI USING WIKI

Regardless of teaching content and pedagogical approaches, instructors are always interested in how to engage all students in active learning and how to motivate students to enhance their problem solving, critical thinking, and collaborative learning skills. Those skills in today's society are recognized as essential and are facilitated when knowledge is linked to and applied in real situations. With social networking tools such as wikis, it is relatively easy for students to collaborate in PBI by presenting their problem-solving process to a wiki and viewing everyone's work. However, many instructors in higher education still rely on traditional instructional tools or simple technology applications such as word processors or presentation software, and rarely use social networking technology tools to design and conduct courses. To demonstrate how wikis could be incorporated to promote learning in higher education, we now summarize the instructional strategies learned from the cases and provide some guidelines for designing a PBI with this Web 2.0 tool. To this end, we clustered the guidelines in a design model: Preparation, Pedagogy, Participation and Assessment, or P3A (see Figure 4.1).

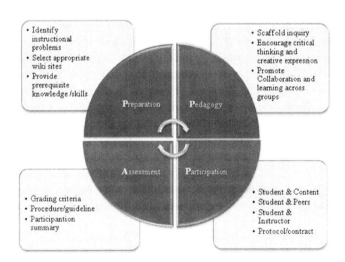

FIGURE 4.1.   PBI design with wikis (P3A design model). This image represents the P3A Design Model for PBI Design using wikis. The P3A model includes Preparation, Pedagogy, Participation, and Assessment.

Preparation of Students for PBI Using Wiki

Unlike the traditional, lecture-based instruction, PBI is a student-centered constructivist learning approach that situates students in a problem context. When instructors design a PBI using a wiki, at the "Preparation" phase, instructors need to identify instructional problems related to learning standards and intended learning objectives. The problems usually represent real-life scenarios and serve to trigger and intrigue the learners.

To support students in taking control of their own learning and to effectively communicate with their group, instructors need to provide directions for their solution-building, communicating, and networking channels, including the selection of appropriate technological tools. There are a variety of Web 2.0 tools that allow students to learn and communicate collaboratively with peers and instructors. Wiki is one of the popular and potentially efficient Web 2.0 tools that can be seamlessly adopted in education settings because of the educational affordances wikis provide. The basic wiki features typically include WYSWYG (*what you see is what you get*) editing, uploading images or files, embedding media, tracking history, RSS feeds, adding pages, and providing template pages. Many wiki hosts such as Wikispaces, PBworks, Wetpaint, Google Sites, and so on are usually open source or of low cost. If universities already use a Course Management System (CMS) like Blackboard, it may offer a wiki element. Most wiki tools are easy to use and provide an option to make the site public or private—only accessible for invited members. As mentioned previously, effective collaboration in PBI requires direct access to a usable knowledge base and easy sharing and tracing of ideas from each individual group member (Savin-Baden & Major, 2004). The inherent features of any wiki offer great potential for meeting these requirements in group work. Nevertheless, a wiki is unable to function as the only communication channel in PBI. In both Cases 2 and 3 when partial or the majority of PBI activity was performed asynchronously, students found it hard to communicate solely with wiki, and they preferred using email/instant messenger as a supplement (Hazari et al., 2009; Zorko, 2009).

After instructors select appropriate wiki tools, instructors should help students to build prerequisite knowledge and skills to perform the learning task with appropriate instructional strategies and technology skills. Problem solving is a highly demanding learning task requiring an array of skills, including analyzing the problem situation; relating, applying, and evaluating existing knowledge/skill to the situation; and identifying and bridging gaps before arriving at a viable solution. Before students start tackling the problems assigned to them, instructors need to make sure students have enough background knowledge and are familiar with the problem-solving techniques. In several of the cases we reviewed in the last section (such as Williams et al., 2010; Robertson, 2008), instructors delivered fundamental content in lectures and tutorials before letting student embark on the PBI journey. In addition, the instructor could also model the inquiry process in PBI with a sample question.

Pedagogical Approaches in Designing Wiki-Supported PBI

PBI allows students to construct knowledge through a variety of learning processes, including inquiry, critical thinking, social, and cognitive collaboration with peers and experts. For such a complicated task, scaffolding is essential. In many of the cases discussed above, wiki was used to assist students' inquiry processes and to facilitate collaboration among peers. For example, instructors can also use a pre-determined template or sidebar in wikis to present problem-solving procedures and useful resource links for conducting research and completing tasks. In addition, facilitators can also continuously update the wikis according to the desired pace and progress of the problem-solving process (Neumann & Hood, 2009). From those cases, wiki appeared to be a nice tool to disseminate such support because the information updated on a wiki is instantly available for students. Scaffold-

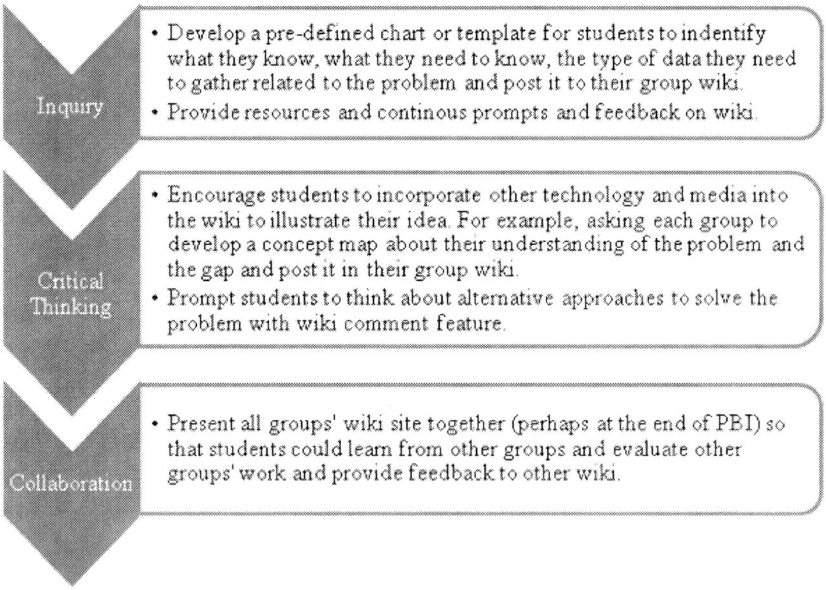

Inquiry
• Develop a pre-defined chart or template for students to indentify what they know, what they need to know, the type of data they need to gather related to the problem and post it to their group wiki.
• Provide resources and continous prompts and feedback on wiki.

Critical Thinking
• Encourage students to incorporate other technology and media into the wiki to illustrate their idea. For example, asking each group to develop a concept map about their understanding of the problem and the gap and post it in their group wiki.
• Prompt students to think about alternative approaches to solve the problem with wiki comment feature.

Collaboration
• Present all groups' wiki site together (perhaps at the end of PBI) so that students could learn from other groups and evaluate other groups' work and provide feedback to other wiki.

FIGURE 4.2. Pedagogical strategies for collaborative PBI using wiki. This figure explains the pedagogical strategies for collaborative PBI using wiki. The pedagogical strategies include inquiry, critical thinking, and collaboration.

ing process could also be achieved by using question prompts and feedback provided on the wiki—usually with the comment feature.

Social constructivism advocates that a co-constructive knowledge-building activity involves both individual and group processes. These combined processes could improve representational artifacts and lead to creative results that would not have been achieved by any single individual alone (Bereiter, 2002). When teachers design a PBI with a wiki, it is imperative for students to share resources, individual perspectives, and solution proposals before reaching a consensus within their group. For this purpose, wiki offers an instrumental platform that upholds equable and instant sharing. In addition, wiki does not prevent group members from using other types of technologies. In fact, the technology fosters the incorporation of various media. Students can easily upload or link to their artifacts created with other technologies including pictures, documents, and videos. For example, instructors can encourage students to express their ideas visually with concept maps, which could also encourage critical thinking and knowledge integration.

Besides learning from one another within each group, wikis can promote learning across groups. In order to ensure that students learn different perspectives from others, teachers may present all wikis at the end of PBI and ask students to identify differences by comparing their wiki with other groups' wikis or provide feedback after they evaluate other groups' work. Figure 4.2 illustrates some pedagogical strategies an instructor can employ to support the collaborative PBI with wikis.

Students' Participations on Wikis

This section discusses three types of student participation on wikis when engaged in PBI activities: (1) students and content, (2) students and peers, and (3) students and instructor. We also explain how instructors could establish protocols and procedures in order to facilitate students' participation on wikis. As discussed in the cases in the section above, wikis enable multi-dimensional interactions among students, instructors, and content (see Figure 4.3).

Interaction Between Student Peers

In a PBI activity, students can only arrive at a viable solution for a problem through peer interaction by negotiating and structuring knowledge. Therefore, students' social and cognitive interactions are crucial for the success of PBI. During PBI processes, all students need to understand the value and purpose of their learning and identify what they need to know regarding the presented problem. After the problem is clearly defined, students in a group can be assigned different roles. In Case 3, the instructor explicitly required role assignment and protocol articulation within each

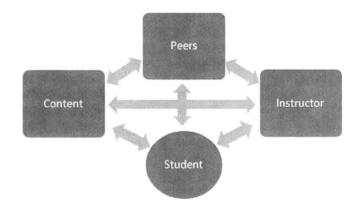

FIGURE 4.3. Interactions in PBI using a wiki. This image indicates different types of student's interactions in PBI using a Wiki: (1) interaction between student and peers, (2) interaction between student and content, (3) interaction between student and content.

group (Hazari et al., 2009). For example, the writer is responsible for preparing a report; the presenter can generate visual forms such as a graph, diagram, concept map, and so on; and the evaluator may check whether their solutions can solve the problem efficiently/effectively and produce the learning outcome desired. Role assignment places students in a more proactive position, and hence promotes engagement with PBI.

To achieve a desired group goal in PBI, students should learn to manage group dynamics more effectively. Establishing practical patterns of communication and coordination is an important aspect of group dynamics (Dyer, 1994). Wikis, with the asynchronous feature, offer students with ample opportunities for interactions with peers, learning content/resources, and the instructor. In addition, understanding of the behavior of other people in groups is another essential aspect of group dynamics (Dyer, 1994). The tracking feature of each individual member's contribution to the problem solution on the wiki provided explicit evidence of his or her thinking processes. In several cases reviewed in last section, students expressed appreciation for the flexible and tracking features of the wiki (Hazari, et al., 2009; Robertson, 2008; Zorko, 2009).

Interaction Between Student and Instructor

In wiki-supported PBI processes, instructors should constantly interact with students and prompt them with different perspectives or alternative solutions. Williams et al. (2010) suggested that instructors/facilitators should assist or direct the groups towards a solution instead of leading the discussion or providing answers to bridge the gaps in their knowledge. If instructors find that a desirable issue eludes students, or an unproductive or even wrong direction emerges from the main problem, instructors may orchestrate their discussions with prompts. Zorko (2009) in Case 2 pointed out that wikis allowed the instructor to offer immediate feedback on students' progress whereas prior to using the wiki, the instructor could not provide prompt comments. In both Cases 3 and 4, timely feedback, provided on the wiki with the comment feature, was found to be a critical factor for students' success. If the instructor's feedback was not provided in a timely manner, students may have gone too far down the wrong path by the time the instructor intervened. However, the quality of interaction between students and instructor would be a big challenge for most instructors. To ensure of the quality of interaction, Williams et al. (2010) stressed the importance of facilitator training before introducing PBI into the curriculum.

Interaction Between Student and Content

In the traditional classrooms, readings and lectures are the most common way for students to interact with content. Instructors usually disseminate instructional resources to support their student learning with or without technology. Web 2.0 tools turn students from passive observers to active creators. Especially with wikis, students need to collectively regenerate learning materials or devise problem solutions by internalizing and articulating content knowledge.

Establishing Protocols

Although wiki tools seem fairly straightforward to set up and use for class projects, users should be aware of some limitations. Since a wiki typically allows only one user to edit it at a time, the instructor should recommend that each group establish participation protocols when using wiki for asynchronous collaboration in PBI processes. For example, instructors may create multiple small groups, ask students in a group to access the wiki by taking turns, or prepare their postings in an alternative software application like word processing programs.

When instructors design a wiki-supported PBI activity, they need to consider the boundary of the learning community based on specific learning tasks and student characteristics. Instructors should determine whether wikis can be accessible by a defined group or the public and who will have the editorship and can make comments. In Case 2, students expressed preference for publishing only the finished product on the wiki; because of the public nature of wikis, students were hesitant to show their work in progress (Zorko, 2009). In addition, when students quote other people's work, they should be aware of copyright and licensing issues. Instructor should also discourage students from publishing inappropriate information or comments on wikis.

Assessment Strategies

In a wiki-supported PBI activity, instructors need to take both formative and summative assessments into consideration in order to measure student problem-solving performances, collaborative behaviors, and self-directed learning skills. To this end, instructors can constantly monitor each group's progress on their wiki and offer comments when needed. The formative assessment, usually content- and strategy-oriented, is geared to provide triggers, content resources, or clarifications to assist students in the PBI processes. It would be beneficial if students are formatively assessed multiple times during the whole PBI process. Students in several cases found such assessing comments motivating (e.g., Zorko, 2009; Williams, et al., 2010).

At the end of the PBI process, instructors conduct the summative assessment to measure students' learning outcome. Although a variety of assessment methods exist, we recommend the following assessment methods instrumental for the summative assessment in PBI using wikis based on the review of the cases above: task performance assessment (group and individual) and self- and peer evaluation (see Table 4.1).

With a traditional collaborative approach, determining the individual contributions to the group assessment tasks has been an issue and a challenge in many classes. However, the tracking history of participations is one most powerful feature of a wiki. The tracking history or participation summary (see Figure 4.4) feature within wikis allows instructors to easily keep up with the change and the author of the revision.

If used properly, wikis can be extremely powerful tools for assessment because instructors can monitor students' participation on wiki. When instructors design assessment criteria or rubrics, factors for consideration

TABLE 4.1. Type of Assessment for PBI Using Wikis

Assessment	Methods
Task performance assessment (group and individual contributions)	While instructors assess the learning performance by each group, they can also check each individual student' contribution to the group work in wiki tools by reviewing the participation statistics.
Peer and self-assessment	Instructors provide guidelines/rubrics for evaluating peer and self-contributions to the group work and review the students' submissions confidentially.

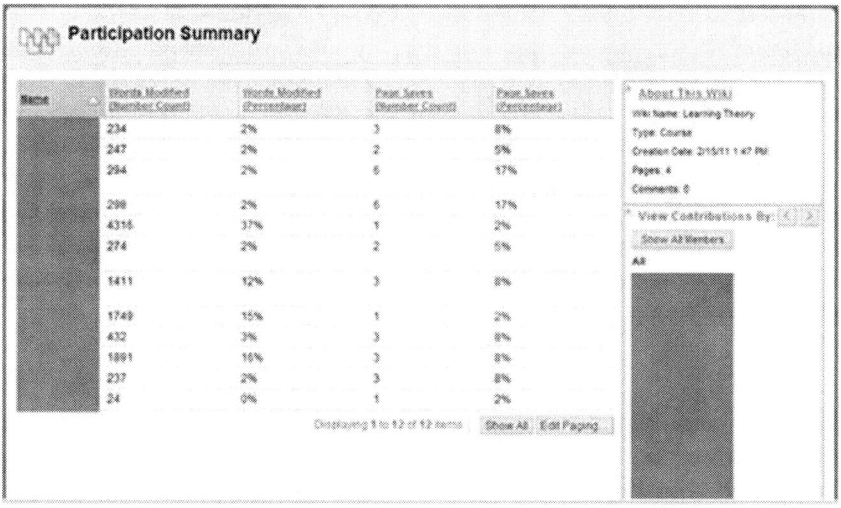

FIGURE 4.4. Participation summary screen on a wiki. This screenshot shows an example of students' participation summary on a wiki including words modified (number count), words modified (percentage), page saved (number count), page saved (percentage) by each contributor.

may include: quality of contribution, quantity/frequency of contribution and professional manner meeting timelines/deadlines. Table 4.2 shows an example of grading criteria.

TABLE 4.2. Students' Contributions Grading Criteria in PBI Using Wikis

Contribution on Wiki	Grading Criteria
Social interaction	Post greeting or topic unrelated to the problem
Task clarification	Ask for clarifications of the assignment, guideline, deadline, etc.
Question	Ask questions related to the problem
Personal opinion	Post personal opinions to the problem without inquiring/searching.
Resources/data	Provide meaningful resources and data related to the main problem by effective inquiring/searching.
Construction of knowledge	Connect the knowledge to resolve the main problem by applying critical thinking skills.
Co-Construction of knowledge	Work with other students collaboratively to find out effective solutions of the main problem.
Reflection	Include insightful self-reflections in the problem solving process.

Instructors are typically the only evaluator of students' learning performance. However, in wiki-supported PBI, it would be a good practice to have the students perform self- and peer-assessment skills. For example, in Case 4 (Williams et al., 2010), each student was asked to rate and rank the contribution of each team member including himself or herself. Additionally, students could give comments about the contributions of a specific group member. The peer assessment was performed three times throughout the semester to guarantee that variations in performance were accounted for. Through peer assessment, students can also learn from reviewing or evaluating others' work.

CONCLUSION

In recent years, higher education has witnessed an increasing emphasis on the use of instructional technology to promote students' problem-solving and critical thinking skills. Collaborative problem-based instruction (PBI) nestles groups of students in a reality-mimic, problematic situation and engages them in a solution-seeking activity. Because of wiki's unique educational affordances, wiki has been heralded as one of the most effective Web 2.0 technologies to promote collaborative learning and it has been, to some extent, used for collaborative problem-solving as indicated by the literature. However, because of the sophistication of the instructional strategy and the novelty of the technology, researchers and practitioners might find it formidable to incorporate the technology into PBI activities. We felt it was imperative to provide a comprehensive body of guidelines for the design and implementation of wiki-supplemented collaborative problem-based instruction.

This chapter reviewed five exemplary cases that engaged students in wiki-supported PBI, showing certain successes of wiki-supported PBI on students' perceptions of learning, attitudes, and course engagement. In addition, this chapter examined the design considerations of using wiki for PBI in great depth and proposed a model, Preparation, Pedagogy, Participation and Assessment (P3A). With this model, we discussed instructional strategies for the design and implementation of PBI. In order to support effective PBI with a wiki tool, instructors should provide templates, resources, guidelines, and immediate feedback; set up protocols for interactions; establish deadlines; and assign roles or responsibilities.

We believe that Web 2.0 can facilitate productive learning in K–12 schools as well as higher education if instructors thoughtfully consider the factors we addressed in this chapter. Although we mainly focused on wiki-supported PBI in higher education, we expect more benefits of Web 2.0 technologies such as wikis, blogs, and social networking sites in classrooms to promote high-quality learning, critical thinking, and collaboration.

REFERENCES

Andrew, T. (2008). *Teaching with Web 2.0: Benefits interactive web technology brings to education.* Retrieved from http://teachingtechnology.suite101.com/article.cfm/teaching_with_web_20

Baird, D. E., & Fisher. M. (2005). Neomillennial user experience design strategies: Utilizing social networking media to support 'always on' learning styles. *Journal of Educational Technology Systems, 34*(1), 5–32.

Barr, R. B., & Tagg, J. (1995). From teaching to learning: A new paradigm for undergraduate education. *Change, 27*(6), 12–25.

Barrows, H. S., & Tamblyn, R. W. (1986). A taxonomy of problem based learning methods. *Medical Education, 20,* 481–486.

Bereiter, C. (2002). *Education and mind in the knowledge age.* Mahwah, NJ: Lawrence Erlbaum Associates.

Boud, D., & Felletti, G. E. (1997). *The challenge of problem-based learning.* London, UK: Kogan-Page.

Dyer, W. (1994). *Team building* (3rd ed.). Upper Saddle River, NJ: Prentice Hall.

Ebersbach, A., Glaser, M., & Heigl, R. (2006). *Wiki: Web collaboration.* Berlin Heidelberg: Springer-Verlag.

Engel, C. E. (1997). Not just a method of learning but a way of learning. In D. Boud & G. Feletti (Eds.), *The challenge of problem based learning* (pp. 17–27). London, UK: Kogan Page.

Esch, C. (2000). Project-based and problem-based: the same or different? *Challenge 2000 multimedia project.* San Mateo, CA: San Mateo County Office of Education.

Hazari, S., North, A., & Moreland, D. (2009). Investigating pedagogical value of wiki technology. *Journal of Information Systems Education, 20*(2), 187–198.

Heycox, K., & Bolzan, N. (1997). Applying problem-based learning in first year social work. In D. Boud & G. Feletti (Eds.), *The challenge of problem based learning* (pp. 186–193). London, UK: Kogan Page.

Hsu, J. (2007). Innovative technologies for education and learning. *International Journal of Information and Communication Technology Education, 3*(3), 70–89.

Konieczny, P. (2007). Wikis and Wikipedia as a teaching tool. *International Journal of Instructional Technology and Distance learning, 4*(1), 15–34.

Neumann, D. L., & Hood, M. (2009). The effects of using a wiki on student engagement and learning of report writing skills in a university statistics course. *Australasian Journal of Educational Technology, 25*(3), 382–398.

Nicol, D., Littlejohn, A., & Grierson, H. (2005). The importance of structuring information and resources within shared workspaces during collaborative design learning. *Open Learning, 20*(1), 31–49.

Raine, D., & Symons, S. (2005). Experiences of PBL in physics in UK higher education. In E. Poikela & S. Poikela (Eds.), *PBL in context: Bridging work and education.* Tampere, Finland: Tampere University Press.

Rhem, J. (1998). Problem based learning: An introduction. *National Teaching and Learning Forum Newsletter, 8*(1). Retrieved from: http://www.ntlf.com/html/pi/9812/pbl_1.htm

Robertson, I. (2008). Learners' attitudes to wiki technology in problem based, blended learning for vocational teacher education. *Australasian Journal of Educational Technology, 24,* 425–441.

Ryan, G. (1997). Ensuring that students develop an adequate, and well-structured, knowledge base. In D. Boud & G. Feletti (Eds.), *The challenge of problem based learning* (pp. 125–136). London, UK: Kogan Page.

Savin-Baden, M., & Major, H. C. (2004). *Foundations of problem-based learning.* Maidenhead, UK: Open University Press.

Uden, L., & Beaumont, C. (2006). *Technology and problem-based learning.* Hershey, PA: Information Science Publishing.

Williams, D. P., Woodward, J. R., Symons, S. L., & Davies, D. L. (2010). A tiny adventure: The introduction of problem based learning in an undergraduate chemistry course. *Chemistry Education Research and Practice, 11*(1), 33–42.

Woods, D. R. (1996). *Problem-based learning: helping your students gain the most from PBL* (3rd ed.). McMaster University: Hamilton. Retrieved May 20, 2011, from http://tp.edu.sg/pbl_donaldwoods.pdf

Zorko, V. (2009). Factors affecting the way students collaborate in a wiki for English language learning. *Australasian Journal of Educational Technology, 25*(5), 645–665.

CHAPTER 5

RECORDED VOICE REFLECTION IN PROBLEM-BASED LEARNING SCENARIOS

Dana A. Tindall and Kay Kyeong-Ju Seo

The advance of Web 2.0 technologies allows instructors a number of ways to teach. Multiple authoring and collaborative student projects stemming from this technology offer a variety of opportunities for problem-based learning (PBL) and associated reflection to be used in education. In this chapter we discuss authentic activity in PBL and typologies of reflection that might stem from those activities. We provide examples aimed at humanities, sociology, and business higher education students. Online externalization tools for reflective dissemination via text-based discussion, blogging, and audio recording are discussed, as well as their similarities, advantages, and limitations. The advantages and theoretical grounding for use of audio recording as a student method of reflection is included with examples of possible use for this type of technology in PBL scenarios.

Designing Problem-Driven Instruction with Online Social Media, pages 87–104
Copyright © 2012 by Information Age Publishing

INTRODUCTION

The advance of newer and better technologies requires that we look to advance their use to align with student needs of the future. The use of voice recording as a tool in problem-based learning (PBL) caters to immediacy as well as the lifestyle of today's learners who spend great amounts of time using technology utilizing it in a form Brown (2000) describes simply as multiprocessing. Students of higher education are faced by technology-based pedagogy in their daily coursework. Course-generated scenarios that require the ability to create digital audio artifacts for an assignment seem a fitting way for higher education instructors to prompt learning using technology. Learning will occur beyond just the course materials; PBL tasks involving audio recording will teach and enable students to communicate fluently in media that can compliment or even replace text. Problem-based learning strategy that utilizes audio recording lends itself well to university-level courses across the spectrum of curricula, from humanities to business education.

The practical ability to create voice recordings has been around since the invention of the phonograph cylinder in 1877 (Mileham, 2009). Early technical advances brought us through a variety of methods up to the ability to record audio on magnetic tape with the first recorders appearing in the late 1940s (Morton, 2006). With the advent of portable tape recorders, the ability to spontaneously record voice became simple, and through increased miniaturization, it became a way to easily record personal notes in the field. Digital audio recording technologies spawned from 1960s development in telephone technologies (Morton, 2006), and great advances in digital memory storage took this one step further. With the 1990s came with the additional advantage of easy electronic transfer of that recorded audio to other forms of storage such as compact discs (Morton, 2006), computer hard drives, and online network servers. High amounts of compact digital memory now allow recording times with miniature mobile devices to go for hours. Capability for easy distribution and sharing of recorded audio has been very much enhanced by this advance of digital technology. Sharing audio files has become not much different than sharing text documents online. The internet fosters interaction; "the web is two way, push and pull" (Brown, 2000, p. 12), and this of course means it can be used as a valuable tool for teaching and learning.

Digital software tools for recording audio are easily found. Several free programs are available on the Internet for quick download and usage. Most computer platforms also include audio recording and editing software in their operational systems. Some current common software programs for sound editing include GarageBand® for Mac, Adobe Audition® for PC, and Audacity®, which works on both Mac and PC platforms (Buffington, 2010). Some of these programs can be rather sophisticated and provide the chance to record and combine several discrete audio tracks together into the same output. A long list of modifications including speed, pitch, and amplitude of the audio can be manipulated by these programs as well. These tools also allow for deleting portions of, or inserting parts of, audio recordings into other stored recordings.

Not all the advances have come in software; aside from the ability to plug a microphone into your computer and record your voice, many other devices offer recording capabilities. Some of those devices are personal digital assistants, cell phones, smart phones, and of course digital audio recorders. Some of these mobile devices even allow transfer to other devices via wireless phone and internet networks; contextual audio recording on the spot and in the field has never been easier.

Voice recording using these devices in a contextual field allows spontaneous active reflection from a learner and the ability to quickly capture thought through the naturalness of the spoken word. The instructor may more easily examine the reflective thought process of the learner through voice inflection (Marriott & Hiscock, 2002), choice of wording, and relative conciseness of thought. In this chapter, we will examine theory, pedagogical reasoning, and strategies for using recorded voice reflection by students in problem-based scenarios. Existing technology tools and some example strategies using recorded audio are discussed, along with issues associated with this process.

WEB 2.0 AND PROBLEM-BASED LEARNING

Web 2.0

Web 2.0 is a term used to describe online social media and interaction. This technology is geared toward active personal and interpersonal engagement both individually and collaboratively. Earlier web technologies were essentially "read only"; the user would find the web resource and glean information. Web 2.0 instead makes the user an author of the media, so these technologies are essentially "read/write" in nature. The user, or in the educational sense the learner, has the capability to seek these media out and go beyond mere passive observation; learners can now input and add their interpretation to what was formally an output-only modality. As stated above, the digital world is not just limited to text input alone: "With the Web, we suddenly have a medium that honors multiple forms of intelligence" (Brown, 2000, p. 12). Pictures, audio, video, and cross hyper-linking to other online resources truly make Web 2.0 into a network of information, all through shared authorship.

There is little agreement as to what Web 2.0 actually is, but it can be defined as "certain forms of activities or practices....[I]t is not a binary function, but rather a question of degree" (Dohn, 2009, p. 345). Indeed, it is a modality for interaction and shared thinking. Latour (1996) states, "For humans it is almost impossible to find an interaction that does not make some appeal to technics...human interaction is most often localized, framed, held in check. By what? By the frame, precisely, which is made up of non-human actors" (p. 238). The non-human actors in this case are the technology tools and artifacts, the frame, offered by Web 2.0.

Pedagogical practices in Web 2.0 can include a wide variety of applications that are all social in nature. Among these are blogs, wikis, media sharing, mashups, synchronous conferencing, and virtual worlds (Vaughn, 2010). The use of Web 2.0 social media as a tool of pedagogy is reliant on the students' continuing and interactive social discourse by way of online mediation. The focus of these technologies is the support of learning by resituating content and practice between formal and informal learning settings. Their use provides acquisition of competencies in the technologies and practices in which they will likely be working beyond their academic tenure (Dohn, 2009).

Problem-Based Learning

Web 2.0, communication channels and open access of resources for student knowledge building and dissemination of learning, forms a useful and adaptable foundation for problem-based learning (PBL). The best practice criteria for digital learning design include the need for PBL modules that will assist in critical thinking as well as help develop core skills (Brittain, Chambers, & Marriott, 1998). Constructivism posits that there is a real world that we experience, and in that world meaning is imposed on us rather than existing independent of us (Duffy & Jonassen, 1992). Meaning then is created internally by forces that are external. Rather than the objectivist funneling of information into a student's head, the learner is an active participant in the learning process by way of contextual exposure to a variety of external stimuli such as media, environmental, social and cultural contacts. Social negation then can be the means for learning and understanding (Vygotsky, 1978). Social negation signals the need for communication and collaboration, and collaboration is "a means of testing ideas and evaluating alternative perspectives" (Duffy & Bednar, 1992, p. 129). Social constructivism then means that learners find and create meaning through societal interaction and placement in an authentic contextual environment such as those seen in PBL.

Social constructivist strategies rely heavily upon collaboration. This can occur online, in a face-to-face setting, or a blend of the two. In any of these settings, collaboration depends upon several factors for success. Connolly, Jones, and Jones (2007) note several of these: Members of collaborative groups are stakeholders in the way the group functions, in terms of individual work load as well as work results. They, as individuals and as group members, must be involved in decision making and role definitions for each member, and they must be able to be flexible and operate formally and informally. They must be clear in defining the goals of the collaboration, developing a common and coherent vision, and keep this in mind through the duration of the collaborative process (Connolly et al., 2007). They are a team, and the team must be placed in some sort of course context that is authentic.

Authentic course activities provide for meaningful learning in that they place the learner in a context similar to what they might experience in the real world. Reeves, Herrington, and Oliver (2002) state that in order to preserve the complexity of real life, the course can be designed as a metaphor based on a realistic context. These authors have identified from research several characteristics as guidelines for authentic activities. They say authentic activities for students are ill-defined and have real-world relevance as they require students to define complex tasks and subtasks for completion over a sustained period of time. The activities provide opportunities to collaborate and reflect on examinations of that task from different perspectives. By way of this process, students can integrate this information to be applied across different domains and subject areas, producing a product coming from multiple and diverse outcomes that are seamlessly integrated with the assessment (Reeves et al., 2002).

Authentic activities then are very closely aligned and fit very well with PBL, which is a pedagogical practice using the reaction to relevant and challenging ill-defined situations to motivate and engage a learner with resources, collaborative thinking, and problem-solving. Learning occurs in this process, which can be transferred forward into eventual real-world practice. Problem-based learning then can be seen as an effective means for experiential and meaningful learning, and it also forms a tool for generation of student reflection and change.

Problem-based learning can include computer simulations, virtual environments, and even be utilized by students working alone (Mercier & Frederiksen, 2007). The students are responsible for developing a position and solution in relation to a presented case, somewhat as if they were working in the real world (Barab & Duffy, 2000). Barrows (2002) describes "keys" to the PBL method, beginning with presenting the learner an ill-structured problem that stimulates inquiry for more information to facilitate resolution. The problems are chosen to align with activities that will be required in the real world. The learners assume the responsibility of their learning and contributions to the task. The instructor becomes a facilitator and works with the learners to construct knowledge in an "adult–adult" type relationship rather than a "parent–child" type relationship (Barrows, 2002).

COMMUNICATION MEANS FOR
PROBLEM-BASED LEARNING

Communication is of course of utmost importance in PBL as active participation, particularly among groups, is needed for group creation of hypotheses, for cause and management of the problem, and for the task of solving the problem. Beyond the importance of peer-to-peer communication in the environment, the instructor or facilitator must above all be in close communicative touch. Monitoring students even in an adult–adult situation requires keeping close tabs. Students without facilitation face the very real prospect of inadvertently going off track as they deal with an ill-defined problem set. Thinking outside of the ordinary is good, but not understanding what the ordinary is can be a catastrophic path toward failure in design and outcomes of the lesson.

Some tool must be available for communication between individual peers and between the learners and the instructor. Records of the group thought can provide a linear path through the problem-solving task with every iteration of the resolution process archived for review and assessment, both formative and summative. There are a variety of online modalities that will facilitate communication and collaboration in PBL. For the most part these are text-based. Text provides a firm communication strategy that can be applied online for asynchronous communication. A value in text-based communication is that it is an archive that can be referenced and reflected upon repeatedly. Creation of text communication, particularly for asynchronous use, may not be the fastest way of expression, but it offers an opportunity for the author to be reflective and thoughtful in applying reasoning to communication. Asynchronous communication does not necessarily depend upon speed of delivery, as it is not conversational in the normative means. It is a slow strategy that allows for cognitive processing and depth of thought.

Discussion Boards

Many university courses commonly use text-based discussion boards for student interaction and for reflection on course materials. Online discussion boards are asynchronous in nature and essentially text-based. As a common element in course management systems (CMS), the discussion board often functions as the mainstay in the communication strategy between learners separated by distance and time. Over a given period, a student will post a reflection on any assigned topic, and other learners within the same class will reply in response. Through this system, group communication and collaborative learning through channeled reflection occurs. The discussion "forum" is defined by a posed question, and all reflection centers and radiates in a linear fashion from and around that question. This seems a logical communication structure for PBL. The posed question becomes the problem, and though a variety of posted "threads" each specific element of the problem is considered; information is disseminated, reflected upon, and refined through a serial process of replies until the problem is resolved.

Blogs

Discussion boards work in a way very similar to blogs; in educational settings in that they allow postings of student reflection. Blogs are one of the most common Web 2.0 social networking tools in the life of today's students and have found their way into educational processes. These tools are blurring the line between popular culture and formalized learning (Conrad, 2008). As a tool in both face-to-face and online coursework, they have functioned successfully as text journals to provide a forum for reflection and feedback (Ellison & Wu, 2008; Ladyshewsky & Gardner, 2008; Shim & Gou, 2009). Research found that students reading other students' blogs perceived them to be educationally valuable (Ellison & Wu, 2008), and they liked the simplicity and the informality of blogging (Xie, Ke, & Sharma, 2008). Blogs are very often used to facilitate reflection in face-to-face, blended-format, and distance education courses. Blogs by nature are collaborative communication tools that can easily be utilized in the creation of PBL projects. The popularity of blogs and their usefulness to instructors and students have caused them to be generally incorporated into online CMS.

Major differences exist between blogs and discussion boards. Where discussion boards are as a rule contained in a closed CMS forum, blogs, unless contained in a CMS or are otherwise restricted, are on the web and are subject to public consumption. Discussion boards are very sequential in nature; threads of thought to be applied to group discussion are posted and replied to in a fashion similar to an outline. The graphic layout of a discussion board actually follows this form. Most discussion boards allow files to be attached to a post, but they are largely ancillary items in the posting, and require the reader to download to view. Blogs, on the other hand, are more organic in nature. Like discussion boards, they are centered around a topic but tend to be more personal and informal in nature. They are most often owned by a person but are visible and are able to be commented on or even edited by others. It is not at all unusual to find rich media such as audio or video along with hyperlinked text embedded directly into the text posting. Students observing blogs are invited in an informal way to interact with the content rather than just respond. A viewer may either post a blog entry directly or comment on another person's posting, depending on the permissions granted by the owner of the blog.

Podcasts and Recorded Audio

Text-based communication tools are indeed important and have always been valuable as they communicate settings and ideas in a symbolic manner via text. Part of this conveyance is facilitated by the dexterity and skill of the writer. Communication, however, can be much richer than ideas described by text alone; they can be thoughts and ideas represented by way of spoken words. The rich and empathetic quality of the voice can more powerfully and personally represent the information conveyed in immediate simple form, or through crafted statement. "Language, articulated sound, is para-mount...thought itself relates in an altogether special way to sound" (Ong, 1982, p. 7). The spoken word is primal and an integral part of our social structure and culture. It conveys empathy and the nature of the individual human experience. This enhanced capability can be facilitated easily by technology by way of podcasts or recorded audio.

Podcasts are essentially recorded materials used for a variety of means. Podcast and audio recording are in many ways seen as interchangeable terms, although there are some distinct differences. *Podcast* is the term used in the educational sense for a largely objectivist technology where lessons are recorded for playback later. Podcasts are audio in nature and are often used to essentially replace text as study guide. Instructors are the common source of educational podcasts, but students can make podcasts singly or as an editorial group as part of an assignment. Oddly podcasts, as they are used in most current pedagogy, would seem constructivist upon first glance, but are in fact behaviorist in nature. They are for the most part just study tools designed for repetitive listening. Podcasts are useful but are inherently not interactive, and as an artifact do not directly support collaboration. They are advantageous in that they can be used for easy retrieval of information and can be used for recording of lectures (Hsu, 2007). Podcasts then are born of a "need for convenience" strategy. A student may not be able to study text while driving or performing some other task, but she can certainly listen as she works. The multitasking nature of students in our time does require such tools, and where there is a need, a technology answer is usually forthcoming. That said, podcasts are not always the best solution for students. A study by Janossy (2007) found only a very small number of his sample used the convenience of listening to a study aid podcast while in transportation, and many found the podcasts boring. The concluding perception of this study was that an increased value for the podcasts is in the possibility for collecting unique content not otherwise available.

If collection of unique information is important, then the greatest potential of podcasting lies in its use as a "vehicle for disseminating learner-generated content" (Lee, McLoughlin, & Chan, 2008, p. 504). Currently, only a limited variety of studies examine learner-created podcasts. Many of these gave learners the opportunity to research and create their own knowledge primarily by creating podcasts of recorded interviews. It should be noted that podcasts also can be used to collect information such as observations, notes, and other relevant information in the field (Armstrong, Tucker, &

Massad, 2009). Student assignments in these studies were generally project-based and involved teamwork. The learners were not dependent on situated action, but were involved in collaboration and "knowledge-building dialog" (Lee et al., p. 510). Because they involved collaboration, these podcast assignments were constructivist in nature. Another example is study by Dale and Povey (2009) where students created podcasts in a tourism management course for teaching the theoretical principals of heritage management. Beyond the podcast, students additionally were asked to compile a reflective blog on their experience of developing podcasts. Many students found the creation of the podcast to increase the intrinsic motivation to research and engage with the activity.

Podcasts and audio recordings are in essence memory tools, and as such they can be empathy-laden archives of collected facts. We can know our culture as well as ourselves best through "stories," whether they be recorded in text or recorded in audio:

> When objects and other external entities are viewed as extension of humanity, the notion of learning as a network formation process becomes more palatable. If knowledge exists in external structures of similar nature, as it exists physically within our minds (distributed, neurologically), then it is possible to ascribe knowledge and learning attributes to the distributed nature of networks formed between people. (Siemens, 2006, p. 29)

We lend our knowledge through stories that we share. The stories are reflection, and collections of such are the basis for newer knowledge creation. Stories are witnesses to personal experience and fact, and for the most part form a reflection that can be used as a departure point for knowledge creation by others. They are drawn upon as a complex narrative of factual knowledge, touched by individual personal interpretation. Because they are digital, they provide themselves to external audiences through an online networked means. Because they are external, they are communication, and thus a tool for collaboration.

It seems fitting that with the technical abilities of a computer and a CMS that spoken language for reflection should be an element in online pedagogy and by extension PBL. It is oral reasoning, a spoken story, that can be deeply reflective, or brief and to the point. The element of empathy comes into play here. Pink (2005) discusses the "Conceptual Age" and the role of empathy: "In a world of ubiquitous information...logic alone won't do. What will distinguish those who thrive will be their ability to understand what makes their fellow woman or man tick, to forge relationships, and to care for others" (p. 66). This seems incredibly realistic as we face a world with instant worldwide communication abilities, particularly those beyond text such as audio and video. Collaborative work depends upon humans, and humans are subject to emotion and empathy that cannot always be deeply divulged in text. The ethnographic researcher Darcy Alexandra (2008) provides for this notion in her studies of Irish immigrants. She seeks to use those immigrants' digital multimedia storytelling to provide a richer more complex version of the normally clinically defined experiences and testimonials—the official descriptors of deep human experience (Alexandra, 2008). It seems only reasonable that the use of multimedia modalities such as audio recording is important to future pedagogical strategy, as they will in fact be the tools of future communication.

Voice recording for online collaborative communication permits an immediacy and convenience that text cannot provide. Aside from just a student-generated answer, it allows groups of learners an ability to assess confidence in their knowledge by judging a response to be vocally concise and directed toward the problem. Additionally, it provides a time-saving way to provide meaningful spoken feedback to and between students. Instructor or peer feedback allows the student to take into account the inflection of the communicant's voice and any deeper empathetic meaning that may be conveyed therein. Voice recording has been found to be effective by instructors to post online comments and feedback to students (Ice, Curtis, Phillips, & Wells, 2007). Past studies have shown voice recordings also used effectively as an audio-based discussion tool for second language learning (McIntosh, Braul, & Chao, 2003) and as a student posting option to study the viability of stimulating discussion and understanding of weekly readings in communications classes (Marriott & Hiscock, 2002). Beyond that, voice recordings have been used from mobile phones to post to a special course discussion board via an intermediate file translation step (Wei, Chen, Wang, & Li, 2007).

Jefferies and Hyde (2009), in their study, used a sample of adult students in higher and continuing education. Volunteer students created periodic diary journals of their learning experiences through a variety of electronic media means, including blogs, audio recording, and video recording over an 18-month period. Interestingly, they found the inclination for the type of diary-creating technology changed over the period of the study; the preference for audio recording increased dramatically as text-based forms dropped off. Audio recording technology became important because it was easy to use, versatile, and mobile. The authors found that the students as they matured over time came to adapt and use technology more. Some students even came to understand that they were increasingly dependent upon technology.

AUDIO RECORDING AS A REFLECTIVE TOOL

Reflection and PBL

There is a strong relationship between reflection and PBL, but they are not the same thing. Mantzoukas (2007) voices concerns that there is a notion that PBL and reflection in higher education are seen by many as "interchangeable concepts" (p. 242). He argues that reflective epistemology is concerned with student-created problem identification and formation, whereas a PBL scenario has defined and formed problems developed by an instructor and provided readymade for the students with a specific outcome in mind. Indeed, because reflection involves a self-transformative relationship to a contextual setting, it can only be facilitated by PBL activity, and then often only if reflection is part of the defined problem task. Reflection is a learned process separate from PBL that can be refined with practice. Reflective skills development occurs through "structured and frequent" use of reflection as part of PBL scenarios and yields students who are more autonomous in their learning and eventual professional practice (Cooke & Matarasso, 2005).

The process of PBL can involve different types of reflection. Williams (2001), applying reflection to PBL in nursing, cites Mezirow (1990) defining reflection as coming in three forms: "content reflection," which asks "what"; "process reflection" that examines "how"; and "premise reflection," the most complex, which asks "why" (p. 29). Mezirow's notion of premise reflection is also known as critical reflection and is "derived from critical theory and the work of Habermas" (Kember, McKay, Sinclair, & Wong, 2008, p. 374). An instance of this typology incorporation is a medical online course for professionals developed by Gonzales and Salmoni (2008). They describe a six-stage process that involves a combination of PBL and reflection, beginning with an explanation of self-practice, analysis and discussion with peers, analysis of accepted standards, a PBL exercise with case studies, further interaction in a group task, and finally reflection.

Strategic use for application of PBL should always consider reflection simply because of its complimentary nature. The two together have the potential to take lessons learned using PBL beyond cursory understanding or simple reflection. It seems reasonable as we have more advanced technological capabilities that we also have potential to expand reflection beyond text to consider audio recording in our PBL teaching strategies.

Audio Recording Technology and Strategy

The ability for students to record voice reflection on a computer is relatively simple. As noted previously, several fairly sophisticated audio recording and editing programs can be downloaded from the internet for free. Computer operating systems additionally provide audio recording programs, and many newer computers go so far as to also contain a built-in microphone and speakers. Mobile technologies such as smart phones provide the ability to record and send audio files. The technology components for educator use of audio recording are very much in place. Adding to the ability to record, audio files can be saved in many different file formats in fidelity resolutions from low to very high; they can also be quickly and easily uploaded to a CMS, a blog, or any other Web 2.0 tool that can embed files.

Audio recording technology can be found built into a CMS. The Blackboard® CMS can function with an additional embedded program, Wimba Voice Board®. The technical ability of this discussion board tool makes posting audio reflection and comments a simple task for the student and instructor. The hosted program interface works inside the CMS, though it is not currently a part of that software package. It looks and functions very much like a common text-based discussion board. A bonus feature of this specific tool is an easy to run "wizard" function for help with initial configuration of the client computer, particularly with the microphone, speakers, and internet connection. Students are able to click on a button to record their voice using a microphone, and then have the ability to listen to what they have recorded and rerecord should they not be satisfied with the earlier attempt. Students may additionally upload recorded audio from another source such as a voice recorder or smart phone. If desired, students may also post accompanying text along with the audio recording. The individual postings are listed sequentially, and if the instructor allows, can be listened and responded to by others recording their own voice comments.

Online discussion boards, even voice discussion boards, function very much like blogs. Because of their ability to contain digital information beyond just text, blogs offer an excellent solution for communication and collaboration strategies that contain audio; voice recordings can very easily be posted to and downloaded from a blog.

The opportunities for using audio recording for a problem-based scenario are wide open. Students of history or sociology might, for instance, be given the problem task of compiling and editing oral histories using a single or several older relatives' stories as recorded source materials (Langhorst, 2008). This could be further complimented by the student inserting his or her own audio commentary to combine these audio clips into a narrative flow. Buffington (2010) suggests having art students create an audio art museum tour, where the scripted and authoritative art historian-toned audio tour is instead replaced with a more informal student-generated conversational approach podcast-steering viewers to works that they as a group, or individually, select from an existing exhibition. Audio recording might also be considered as a supplemental element in other problem-based strategies such as webquests. In this case, student groups may be required to record, source from the web, or edit together audio to supplement the other project requirements. Even simple team activities, such as a biology-oriented educational scavenger hunt in a botanical garden or zoo, could utilize audio recording as a reporting and question-generating strategy.

Procedures to use the voice board or audio in a blog as a strategy for PBL may include a reflective component. As a PBL home assignment, an example could be a complex special education classroom scenario in which a specific student, or group of students, is having problems and is causing difficulty and disrupting the rest of the class. The problem might be presented to students as a description of this scenario via text or audio. A more advanced step in this scenario might be to even show students a posted online video clip of the situation. The instructor would then prompt them to audio-record themselves immediately discussing the situation and offering a solution along with a reflection on their justifications. This audio can then be uploaded to the source blog for other students to download, review, and respond. The audio recording in this case allows for spontaneity of response and a chance for other students and the instructor to discern the tone of the student's inflection—that is, the emotional aspect contained in the audio response to the problem. The advantage of using voice recording in this particular case is that it in many ways parallels the real-world problem scenario. The assessment of student responses could allow the instructor to additionally draw conclusions based on the length of response and the ability to respond in a concise and confident manner.

Using recorded audio communication provides guidance in role-playing scenarios or scenarios where time-constraints are part of the problem. How do business instructors judge and assess a student's or group of students' ability to "think on their feet" in an asynchronous environment? Audio recording forms a solution in that it is a time-based medium. An example might be teams of business students working through an ill-structured problem of dealing with an emotional client that keeps changing the rules, or perhaps a client that provokes an ethics-challenging scenario. The instructor role-playing the problem client posts the problem, possibly in audio, to the students, and they respond with an audio recording. The instructor then somehow modifies or confounds the problem in another posting and the students respond again. The blog time-stamps the postings and the instructor can judge the speed of the students' problem-solving reaction as well as the emotional tone of their voices.

Audio recording, as mentioned above, inherently involves emotion in a more pure form than text. A problem assignment that requires deeper critical reflection seems a wonderful target for such a strategy. University sociology or psychology students are given the problem of visiting a local bar, examining, and audio reflecting on-site via their mobile device their reactions to that culture. They can then later reflect again on what gender and sexual issues were present, what they felt about them, and how individuals and institutions should deal with these issues. One more example might be art students given the task of visiting a piece of artwork they personally find challenging and reflecting on-site on the context in which the artwork is placed, their immediate reactions at the time, and what they feel the artist intended. All of these recordings then may be reviewed for later critical reflection either in text or in audio. Active reflections as audio-recorded memories are available from which students can later reflect again.

Problems and Issues

As with many online pedagogical strategies, the student and teacher are dependent on the technology working correctly. Technology issues may present problems and add a layer of stress. Technology continues to get better over time, but there will likely always be some sort of problem issue. This is not to mention student-developed phobias concerning technology assignments. This occurs particularly when an important grade depends heavily upon the technology working correctly. Audio posting within a CMS or blog depends on internet connection speeds for uploads and downloads of files, which can occasionally cause problems because of bandwidth and size. Students may also have troublesome older computers, or intermittent internet connections, and they may have software and hardware difficulties with the recording program. A learning and acclimation curve must be considered by the instructor. It is also of great importance that students and teachers have some sort of training for use of the program so that the software and hardware issues do not interfere in the teaching and learning process.

An interesting problem that may appear is students not liking the sound of their own recorded voice, or their wording choices. This has on occasion caused stress and a perceived need by students to rerecord postings, sometimes several times over. Marriott and Hiscock (2002) note occurrences in their study where students are not comfortable with the sound of their own voices. Our interview data also showed that besides this problem, some students may additionally be stressed by a change from text-based to voice-based reflection. If the audio recordings are to be posted for discussion, students may be tempted to write the reflection and then read their postings verbatim or instead write a list of prompts and thoughts to assist in their voice posts. Though some issues exist, we found that the students for the most part thought the notion of voice posting was good, but felt they needed a period of acclimation before coming to a comfort level with the technology. This is not dissimilar to some of the findings of Marriott and Hiscock (2002).

CONCLUSION

The use of voice recording in problem-based learning caters to situational immediacy as well as the multitasking lifestyle of today's higher education millennial learners who spend great amounts of time using Web 2.0 tools. Voice recording allows spontaneous reflection from a learner. The ability to quickly capture thought through the naturalness of the spoken word allows an instructor to more easily examine the reflective thought process of the learner through voice inflection, choice of wording, and relative conciseness of thought. Additionally, the now almost ubiquitous use of mobile devices that allow voice recording can be taken advantage of by instructors wishing to put students in a contextual real-world situation to let them capture their problem-solving ideas and reflections immediately. These reflections can be used for later educational activity, further deeper reflection in text or audio, and instructor analysis.

The advance of newer and better technology requires we look to leverage its use for alignment with student needs of the future. "Research evidence to date indicates that a proportion of young people are highly adept with technology and rely on it for a range of information gathering and communication activities" (Bennett, Maton, & Kervin, 2008, p. 778). Millennial students multitask (Brown, 2000), and they are attracted by design and playfulness. These students seem a natural fit for Pink's (2005) version of the "Conceptual Age" where his terms of the senses of "story, empathy, and meaning" come into play. Audio recording as an element for problem-based scenarios seems a likely way to realistically engage students. It fits well with learners of today and the future world they face. It allows educators to be able to meaningfully assess their students' competence for a world into which they will go and eventually lead.

REFERENCES

Alexandra, D. (2008). Digital storytelling as transformative practice: Critical analysis and creative expression in the representation of migration in Ireland. *Journal of Media Practice, 9*(2), 101–112. doi:10.1386/jmpr.9.2.101_1

Armstrong, G. R., Tucker, J. M., & Massad, V. J. (2009). Interviewing the experts: Student produced podcast. *Journal of Information Technology Education, 8,* IIP-79; IIP-90.

Barab, S. A. & Duffy, T. M. (2000). From practice fields to communities of practice. In D. H. Jonassen & S. H. Land (Eds.) *Theoretical foundations of learning environments* (pp. 25–55). Mahwah, NJ: Lawrence Erlbaum Associates.

Barrows, H. (2002). Is it truly possible to have such a thing as dPBL? *Distance Education, 23*(1), 119–122. doi:10.1080/01587910220124026

Bennett, S., Maton, K., & Kervin, L. (2008). The 'digital natives' debate: A critical review of the evidence. *British Journal of Educational Technology, 39*(5), 775–786. doi:10.1111/j.1467-8535.2007.00793.x

Brittain, M., Chambers, M., & Marriott, P. (1998, June). *Design considerations in the development and delivery of digital learning media.* Paper presented at the ED-MEDIA/ED-TELECOM 98 World Conference on Educational Multimedia and Hypermedia & World Conference on Educational Telecommunications, Freiburg, Germany.

Brown, J. S. (2000). Growing up digital. *Change, 32*(2), 10.

Buffington, M. L. (2010). Podcasting possibilities for art education. *Art Education, 63*(1), 11–16.

Connolly, M., Jones, C., & Jones, N. (2007). Managing collaboration across further and higher education: A case in practice. *Journal of Further & Higher Education, 31*(2), 159–169. doi:10.1080/03098770701267630

Conrad, D. (2008). Reflecting on strategies for a new leaning culture: Can we do it? *Journal of Distance Education, 22*(3), 157–161.

Cooke, M., & Matarasso, B. (2005). Promoting reflection in mental health nursing practice: A case illustration using problem-based learning. *International Journal of Mental Health Nursing, 14*(4), 243–248. doi:10.1111/j.1440-0979.2005.00388.x

Dale, C., & Povey, G. (2009). An evaluation of learner-generated content and podcasting. *Journal of Hospitality, Leisure, Sport & Tourism Education, 8*(1), 117–123. doi:10.3794/johlste.81.214

Dohn, N. (2009). Web 2.0: Inherent tensions and evident challenges for education. *International Journal of Computer-Supported Collaborative Learning, 4*(3), 343–363. doi:10.1007/s11412-009-9066-8

Duffy, T. M., & Bednar, A. K. (1992). Attempting to come to grips with alternative perspectives. In T. Duffy (Ed.), *Constructivism and the technology of instruction: A conversation* (pp. 129–135). Hillsdale, NJ: Lawrence Erlbaum Associates.

Duffy, T. M., & Jonassen, D. H. (1992). Constructivism: New implications for instructional technology. In T. Duffy & D. Jonassen (Eds.), *Constructivism and the technology of instruction: A conversation* (pp. 1–16). Hillsdale, NJ: Lawrence Erlbaum Associates.

Ellison, N., & Wu, Y. (2008). Blogging in the classroom: A preliminary exploration of student attitudes and Impact on comprehension. *Journal of Educational Multimedia and Hypermedia, 17*(1), 99–122.

Gonzalez, M. L., & Salmoni, A. J. (2008). Online problem-based learning in postgraduate medical education—Content analysis of reflection comments. *Teaching in Higher Education, 13*(2), 183–192. doi:10.1080/13562510801923302

Hsu, J. (2007). Innovative technologies for education and learning. *International Journal of Information and Communication Technology Education,* 70–89. doi:10.4018/jicte.2007070107

Ice, P., Curtis, R., Phillips, P., & Wells, J. (2007). Using asynchronous audio feedback to enhance teaching presence and students' sense of community. *Journal of Asynchronous Learning Networks, 11*(2), 3–25.

Janossy, J. (2007). Engaging the learner. In *Proceedings of the 12th Annual Instructional Technology Conference.* Retrieved from http://eric.edu.gov.proxy.libraries.uc.edu/PDSF/ED496202.pdf

Jefferies, A., & Hyde, R. (2009). Listening to the learners' voices in HE: How do students reflect on their use of technology for learning? *Electronic Journal of e-Learning, 7*(2), 119–126.

Kember, D., McKay, J., Sinclair, K., & Wong, F. K. Y. (2008). A four-category scheme for coding and assessing the level of reflection in written work. *Assessment & Evaluation in Higher Education, 33*(4), 369–379. doi:10.1080/02602930701293355

Ladyshewsky, R. K., & Gardner, P. (2008). Peer assisted learning and blogging: A strategy to promote reflective practice during clinical fieldwork. *Australasian Journal of Educational Technology, 24*(3), 241–257.

Langhorst, E. (2008). Golden oldies: Using digital recording to capture history. *School Library Journal, 54*(3), 50–53.

Latour, B. (1996). On interobjectivity. *Mind, Culture & Activity, 3*(4), 228–245.

Lee, M. J. W., McLoughlin, C., & Chan, A. (2008). Talk the talk: Learner-generated podcasts as catalysts for knowledge creation. *British Journal of Educational Technology, 39*(3), 501–521. doi:10.1111/j.1467-8535.2007.00746.x

Mantzoukas, S. (2007). Reflection and problem/enquiry-based learning: Confluences and contradictions. *Reflective Practice, 8*(2), 241–253. doi:10.1080/14623940701289311

Marriott, P., & Hiscock, J., (2002). Voice vs. text-based discussion forums: An implementation of Wimba Voice Boards. In G. Richards (Ed.), *Proceedings of world conference on e-learning in corporate, government, healthcare, and higher education 2002* (pp. 640–646). Chesapeake, VA: AACE.

McIntosh, S., Braul, B., & Chao, T. (2003). A case study in asynchronous voice conferencing for language instruction. *Educational Media International, 40*(1), 63–73.

Mercier, J., & Frederiksen, C. H. (2007). Individual differences in graduate students' help-seeking process in using a computer coach in problem-based learning. *Learning and Instruction, 17*(2), 184–203. doi:DOI: 10.1016/j.learninstruc.2007.01.013

Mezirow, J. (1990) *Fostering critical reflection in adulthood.* San Francisco, CA: Jossey-Bass.

Mileham, R. (2009). Sounds of history. *Engineering & Technology 4*(18), 22–24. doi:10.1049/et.2009.1802

Morton, D. (2006). *Review of the history of technologies for recording music: Tape recording and studios.* Retrieved from http://www.recording-history.org/HTML/musictech6.php

Ong, W. J. (1982). *Orality and literacy: The technologizing of the word.* New York, NY: Methuen.

Pink, D. H. (2005). *A whole new mind: Moving from the information age to the conceptual age.* New York, NY: Riverhead Books.

Reeves, T. C., Herrington, J., & Oliver, R. (2002). Authentic activities and online learning. In A. Goody, J. Herrington, & M. Northcote (Eds.), *Quality conversations: Research and development in higher education, 25* (pp. 562–567). Jamison, ACT: HERDSA. Retrieved from http://elrond.scam.ecu.edu.au/oliver/2002/Reeves.pdf

Shim, J. P., & Guo, C. (2009). Weblog technology for instruction, learning, and information delivery. *Decision Sciences Journal of Innovative Education, 7*(1), 171–193.

Siemens, G. (2006). *Connectivism: Learning theory or pastime for the self-amused?* Retrieved from http://www.elearnspace.org/Articles/connectivism_self-amused.htm

Vaughan, N. (2010). Student engagement and web 2.0: What's the connection? *Education Canada, 50*(2), 52–55.

Vygotsky, L. (1978). *Mind and society.* Cambridge, MA: Harvard University.

Wei, F., Chen, G., Wang, C., & Li, L. (2007). Ubiquitous discussion forum: Introducing mobile phones and voice discussion into a web discussion forum. *Journal of Educational Multimedia and Hypermedia, 16*(2), 125–140.

Williams, B. (2001). Developing critical reflection for professional practice through problem-based learning. *Journal of Advanced Nursing, 34*(1), 27–34.

Xie, Y., Ke, F., & Sharma, P. (2008). The effect of peer feedback for blogging on college students' reflective learning processes. *Internet and Higher Education, 11*(1), 18–25.

CHAPTER 6

USING ONLINE SOCIAL MEDIA TO FACILITATE CLINICAL REASONING IN ENTRY LEVEL OCCUPATIONAL THERAPY STUDENTS

Marlene Joy Morgan and Amy Frey Gerney

The development of clinical reasoning skills in entry-level occupational therapy students is a vital yet challenging component of occupational therapy education. While occupational therapy educators have always been challenged to facilitate clinical reasoning, the integration of technology and social media has opened up unique possibilities for this process to be more effective, creative, and efficient. Specifically, the integration of online social media into today's occupational therapy classroom has allowed us to design learning experiences that approach or mimic real-world scenarios. This chapter provides an overview of how social media can be used as a strategy for facilitating clinical reasoning skills in entry-level occupational therapy students. The YouTube video serves as a catalyst for the interaction between the student and the instructor that results in the effective development of an intervention plan.

Designing Problem-Driven Instruction with Online Social Media, pages 105–124
Copyright © 2012 by Information Age Publishing
105

INTRODUCTION

Technology is providing us with opportunities to create more dynamic learning environments to enable students to become competent professionals in occupational therapy. This chapter provides background to clinical reasoning and highlights a case example of one approach for moving students to become competent in this process. The overarching goal of occupational therapy as a profession is "to support the health and participation of people in life through engagement in occupation" (American Occupational Therapy Association [AOTA], 2008, p. 626). An individual's occupations can simply be described as those activities that he wants to do, enjoys doing, or has to do. Occupations may include travelling, reading, photography, teaching, and many other activities that individuals engage in to create and structure a meaningful life. When an individual's occupations are disrupted due to delayed development, a disabling condition, or environmental barrier, quality of life may be compromised (Yerxa, 1992). Occupational therapists move to help develop or restore occupations in the lives of the clients that they serve (Fidler, 2003). Best practice in occupational therapy may be described as individual, client-centered, holistic and humanistic (AOTA, 2008). It is the use of occupation, or meaningful activity as both an intervention and an outcome that defines and differentiates occupational therapy from other health professions and ensures that occupational therapy intervention promotes health and participation (Amini, 2010).

The practice of occupational therapy today is a complex process. It requires the experienced and emerging clinician to integrate knowledge of the anatomical and physiological foundations of behavior, an in-depth knowledge of occupations across the lifespan, and the impact of disabling conditions on independence, function, and quality of life (Hinojosa, 2007). Occupational therapists provide services in a variety of settings and contexts. These include rehabilitation hospitals, schools, long-term care facilities, home care, and community-based programs (Hinojosa, 2007). Occupational therapy interventions may be designed for individuals, groups, or populations. Careful examination of current occupational therapy curricula nationwide reveals that each of these foundational knowledge and practice areas are systematically addressed (AOTA, 2007). Occupational therapy accreditation standards require that students engage in a curriculum that provides them with theoretical and practical skills needed to design and deliver occupational therapy interventions as well as an understanding of the settings in which services are provided (AOTA, 2007; Baum, 2007; Fidler, 2003). Whether they are providing services in institutional or community settings, in a group or individually, occupational therapists are required to collect, analyze, and integrate both observational and evaluative data. This data set is used to design intervention plans and strategies that will facilitate meaningful participation and advance the quality of life for clients. Experienced educators know that observation and evaluation data must be supplemented with an understanding of each client's personal context (Baum, 2007). The combination of observation, evaluation, and context facilitate problem solving and the development and implementation of successful occupational therapy interventions (Baum, 2007).

Clinical Reasoning

Clinical reasoning is a complex process that is central to the practice of occupational therapy, but not readily visible to the learner. The manner in which experienced clinicians engage in the clinical reasoning process has been described and operationalized in the literature (Mattingly & Fleming, 1994; Schell, 2009). Mattingly and Fleming (1994) identified and described four components of clinical reasoning in occupational therapy: procedural, interactive, conditional, and narrative. Procedural reasoning is based on facts. It occurs when the therapist reflects on the information that is available and considers which evaluations and/or interventions are most likely to successfully address the client's problems. Examples of information that may be integrated into the procedural reasoning process are diagnosis, tests and measures, and specific intervention strategies. Interactive reasoning occurs during the therapeutic process. It is concerned with the best approach to communicate with clients in an attempt to understand them. Unlike procedural reasoning that is based on facts, interactive reasoning is intuitive. Conditional reasoning extends beyond a basic knowledge of a condition or diagnosis. It also extends beyond the client's capabilities. Using conditional reasoning, the therapist attempts to understand how the condition and capabilities impact the client's social life, leisure, or overall self-concept. Conditional reasoning allows the therapist to understand what life was like for the client before a disabling condition and how it may affect his or her future. Narrative reasoning is more than the story of the client's life. It involves an appreciation and understanding of the disability as an illness experience and how the condition will affect the story of the client's life (Mattingly & Fleming, 1994).

Clinical reasoning requires each student to combine knowledge of theory and clinical conditions with the client's personal experiences and goals. The evaluation, interventions, and outcomes of occupational therapy are viewed as interacting determinants of one another. Successful application of theory to practice requires that occupational therapists use abstract skills such as critical thinking, clinical reasoning, and clinical problem solving (Baum, 2007; Hinojosa, 2007; Fidler, 2003). The simultaneous employment of procedural, conditional, narrative, and interactive aspects of the clinical reasoning process requires the therapist to interweave theoretical knowledge of disabling conditions with the individual client's aspirations and personal experience in order to create a relevant and viable treatment program (Mattingly & Fleming, 1994; Schell, 2009).

Clinical Reasoning: Progression from Novice to Expert

The skills and strategies that students learn to define and apply in the clinical reasoning process are fundamental to their future practice as occupational therapists. Early in their education, students in an occupational therapy curriculum begin the journey from novice to expert. The hallmark of this progression is an increase in the efficiency of the clinical reasoning process—the speed, flexibility, and accuracy with which contextual data, clinical problem definition, evaluation, and the design of the intervention plan is integrated and implemented. The keys to expert performance are experience, organization of knowledge, efficient gathering and organization of data, and reflection (Mattingly & Fleming, 1994). The primary task as one progresses toward expertise is not only to amass knowledge, but also to develop increasingly more efficient strategies for organizing and manipulating that knowledge for problem solving (Bruer, 1993; Lave & Wenger, 1991). The traditional method of trans-generational transmission of knowledge in occupational therapy has been based on a cognitive apprenticeship model, in which the expert clinician "makes thinking visible" to the novice (Collins, Brown, & Holm, 1991, p. 6). Modeling, scaffolding, fading, and coaching are the components of cognitive apprenticeship and represent a progression from demonstrated problem solving, to guided problem solving, and then to independent problem solving. Based on the authors' professional experience, this has traditionally been done by providing case studies with predetermined intervention strategies. These are presented as exemplars in texts currently used in occupational therapy curricula. Current authors and editors of frequently used texts such as Pendelton & Schultz-Krohn (2010), Trombly & Radomski (2008), and Case-Smith (2009) have all included fully developed case studies for their texts. Students are encouraged to study these case studies as models for the development of their own reasoning skills. The novice to expert strategy can approach clinical reasoning development in a more dynamic way. First, the instructor models the target process, often showing the student what to do. Then, the instructor provides a scaffold or support as the novice carries out a task. The level of support can vary from carrying out a task with the student to giving occasional hints as to what to do next. Fading refers to the gradual removal of support as the student assumes more and more responsibility. Coaching is an ongoing effort by the expert to oversee the novice's learning by choosing and structuring tasks, providing hints, diagnosing problems, offering encouragement, and giving feedback (Collins et al., 1991).

Metacognitive strategies, such as conceptual frameworks, help to enhance expert thought processes and provide a tangible model of expert thinking for the novice (Bruer, 1993; West, Farmer & Wolff, 1991). This iterative process assists the student to become more aware of efficient methods for ordering and using information for more independent problem-solving (Lave & Wenger, 1991; Resnick, 1987; West et al., 1991).

Teaching strategies used to facilitate clinical reasoning in occupational therapy curricula mirror the development process of novice to expert. From this literature some important concepts can be gleaned and applied. These include: making thinking visible, providing appropriate support, structuring tasks, providing hints, offering encouragement, providing formative feedback, providing a conceptual framework, facilitating efficient methods for ordering, and using information and encouraging reflection (Baum, 2007).

Teaching Clinical Reasoning

The development and integration of clinical case studies into occupational therapy grew from their successful use in medical education. Early in the development and history of clinical reasoning, Neistadt, Wright, and Mulligan (1998) described the use of paper based cases that were developed specifically to facilitate the clinical reasoning process in entry- level occupational therapy students. They concluded that the clinical reasoning case studies were effective because they provided students with a holistic picture of the client and his or her occupational therapy treatment. The clinical reasoning case studies also were successful because they were designed to model the process by organizing information according to the subset of clinical reasoning skills (procedural, interactive, conditional or narrative). Historically, various types of case studies have been used in occupational therapy education. These have included written paper cases, videotapes, simulated clients, and real life scenarios.

Problem-based learning has been integrated into selected entry-level occupational therapy curricula. Occupational therapy educators have examined the effectiveness of problem based learning in the development of the clinical reasoning process. Scaffa and Wooster (2004) conducted a study to determine the effects of a course designed with problem-based learning strategies to develop clinical reasoning skills in occupational therapy students. Results indicated that a short and intensive course structured in a problem-based format can significantly facilitate the clinical reasoning skills in entry-level occupational therapy students. In a study of senior-level occupational therapy students, Neistadt (1999) demonstrated that using a clinical reasoning thinking frame to organize the process was an effective way to help entry-level students to learn and apply the concepts.

Table 6.1 presents a sample thinking frame developed and used currently by Marlene Morgan to help students organize and process the data required to make informed decisions and plan meaningful treatment (M.J.

TABLE 6.1.   Case Study Development—Clinical Reasoning Process

To design an occupational therapy intervention for an individual client, group or population consider the following:

1. Provide a short synopsis of the diagnosis or condition or problem.

2. Where are occupational therapy services (OT) typically provided to this population?

3. What are the sociopolitical considerations (laws, payment sources, family and cultural considerations)?

4. What lifestyle/lifespan issues may the client face?

5. Using referral sources and data collected, how would you define the focus of OT?

6. How do you establish goals for the intervention?

7. How will you design intervention based on a theoretical framework and goals?

8. How will you evaluate progress?

9. How will you determine that change or termination of treatment is warranted?

10. What will an action plan look like?

    a. Long Term Goals

    b. Short Term Goals

    c. Occupations Addressed

    d. Therapist Strategies

    e. Rationale for Activity Choice

    f. Activity Description (preparatory/ adjunctive/ purposeful/ occupation)?

11. What resources are available to clients and their families?

Morgan, 2005 ©

Morgan, personal communication, August 6, 2010). Utilization of the thinking frame leads the student to design specific occupational therapy interventions that are client specific and goal directed as seen in Table 6.2.

Hammel, Royeen, Bagatell, Jensen, Loveland, & Stone (1999) studied occupational therapy students' perceptions of problem-based learning across an entry-level occupational therapy curriculum. Students reported that a problem-based approach contributed to their development of information management, critical reasoning, communication, and team building.

Neistadt and Smith (1997) examined the effect of a "classroom as clinic" format using videotaped evaluations on students' reasoning skills. Results of the study suggested that to be truly effective, videotapes needed to be combined with mentoring and coaching in problem definition and problem solving.

VanLeit (1995) integrated clinical reasoning with problem-based learning by describing the use of the case-based method to develop clinical reasoning skills in the context of problem-based learning. Students were presented with cases in a variety of formats: paper, videotape, simulated cases,

TABLE 6.2.   Case Study Development—Activity Description

Case Study Development—Clinical Reasoning Process—Activity Description		
Related Goal:		
Activity Name:		
Materials and Supplies	**Positioning Considerations**	**Steps to Activity Completion**
Therapist's Strategies	**Parameters to Monitor**	**Rationale for Activity Choice**
Suggestions for Upgrading	**Suggestions for Downgrading**	**Feedback**

Morgan, 2005 ©

and real clients. Lysaght and Bent (2005) conducted a study to compare four different styles of presentations in a course in an occupational therapy curriculum designed to develop clinical reasoning skills. Cases were presented to students using printed text, videotapes, live client interviews, and CD-ROM. Both the pedagogical and practical standpoints were investigated. Results indicated that the choice of modality did not have an impact on students' ability to meet course objectives related to clinical reasoning. However, students reported that CD-ROM was the format that allowed for the most relevant information to be conveyed and the highest quality learning experience (Lysaght & Bent, 2005). Vroman and MacRae (1999) challenged the profession to conduct research studies designed to identify approaches and instruments that are easy to use and that measure clinical reasoning. They argued that the traditional methods of evaluation such as the pass rate on national certification examinations may not demonstrate the multidimensional learning and cognitive growth acquired in problem-based leaning (Vroman & MacRae, 1999).

Contemporary scholars and educators in occupational therapy have commented on the importance of the development of clinical reasoning skills in new professionals. Hinojosa (2007) argued that occupational therapy students must learn to solve problems in a timely, efficient and cost effective manner. They caution that this generation may reason differently due to their experiences with technology and life experiences (Hinojosa, 2007). Occupational therapy educators must develop teaching strategies and styles that are consistent with these students. Courses and curricula must incorporate active learning models that focus more on reasoning and less on knowledge and specific techniques (Baum, 2007; Hinojosa, 2007).

USING SOCIAL MEDIA TO FACILITATE THE DEVELOPMENT OF CLINICAL REASONING

The development of online education challenges instructors to reflect on and re-evaluate course content and formats in light of expanded pedagogical options. Instructors in occupational therapy have benefitted from information related to the development of online courses and content modules. Since there is a "greater need to align the student assessment activities with the course objectives and to focus more on discipline-specific inquiry rather than just covering course content" (Garrison & Vaughan, 2008, p. 62), today's educators can benefit from the rich opportunities offered by the creative use of technology. "The challenge is to imagine the integration of approaches and media to most effectively and efficiently achieve the intended learning processes and outcomes" (Garrison &Vaughan, 2008, p. 48). Through the use of this creative process, it is important to be mindful that the course objectives should drive the use of the technology rather than vice versa. There are benefits and draw backs to both the online environment and the face to face classroom and the objectives need to be considered when designing any learning experience. The challenge of creating an environment where students can move from novice to expert can be met by thoughtfully selecting and implementing effective technology tools. Best practice in distance education supports the selection of technology to help meet course objectives.

Most colleges and universities provide instructors with access to an online learning platform such as BlackBoard or Angel. Researchers have begun to examine online learning from the perspective of both the instructor and student and have described strategies unique to this medium. Hatziapostolou and Paraskakis (2010) reported that the effectiveness of formative feedback could be maximized if it was communicated to the student's learning space, an environment where all learning material and resources of a particular lesson reside. Heinrich, Milne, and Moore (2009) and Juwah, Macfarlane-Dick, Matthew, Nicol, and Smith (2004) advocated the use of an online journal within a course management system to allow the instructor and student an easy visual of drafts with feedback in an organized fashion in one location. The online journal also provides an efficient method to manage multiple assignments and archives the student's work. Both the student and instructor can see clearly the extent to which the student is able to understand and internalize the feedback that was given.

Based on the literature, the authors developed a checklist that was used to guide the development of experiences that engaged students in the clinical reasoning process (Baum, 2007; Bruer, 1993; Collins et al., 1991; Hi-

TABLE 6.3. Instructor's Inquisition

Instructional development challenges may be met by answering "yes" to each of the following questions as the case studies are developed and tested:

1. Are there opportunities for the student to develop skills and expertise in all levels of the clinical reasoning process (procedural, interactive, conditional and narrative)?

2. Does the instructor have opportunities to interact with students in a manner that facilitates their movement from novice to expert?

    a. Does the instructor mentor the clinical reasoning process?

    b. Does the instructor provide formative feedback?

    c. Is it clear that the student understands the content and nature of the feedback?

    d. Is there opportunity for the student to develop as independent thinkers (ie. Is there more than one "right answer" to the case?)

3. Do students have the opportunity to reflect on their decisions?

4. Do student have the opportunity to critique and evaluate themselves and their decisions?

5. Do students meet the course objectives from the instructor's perspective?

6. Do students perceive that they have met the course objectives?

7. Does completion of the case move students forward in their clinical reasoning skills and provide a foundation for future practice?

nojosa, 2007; Lave & Wenger, 1991; Mattingly & Fleming, 1994; Resnick, 1987; West et al., 1991). The authors propose these questions to provide structure to the design of the learning experience. Each of these questions as outlined in Table 6.3 was considered in the development of the following learning experience, which was designed to allow the students to move from novice to expert with their clinical reasoning skills.

The Assignment

Students were introduced to the intervention planning process and given a grading rubric that articulated the standards or assignment exemplar. Making sure that the students understood the learning objectives for the assignment, and the criteria for success, was critical to empowering students to be self-regulated learners (Nicol & MacFarlane-Dick, 2006). The technology allowed the instructor the "opportunity for a complex weaving of learning activities and techniques from a full spectrum of possibilities" (Garrison & Vaughan, 2008, p. 33), and from these possibilities, factual fiction was used to combine a real client, Dan, with realistic yet fictional data.

Meet Dan

Students in an entry-level master's degree program in occupational therapy (delivered in a blended learning environment) are first introduced to

Students in an entry-level master's degree program in occupational therapy (delivered in a blended learning environment) are first introduced to Dan, a college professor who has multiple sclerosis, and his wife Colleen, by way of a YouTube video (Figure 6.1) imbedded in the assignment area of the course management system. This YouTube video shows an individual who is very passionate about his work as a photographer and university professor. He and his wife discuss the changes that they have made in their life as a result of multiple sclerosis. The students' therapeutic relationship with him begins with clinical observations as they critically observe and analyze (AOTA, 2008) this couple via this social network and then move into a more private space of a course management system (BlackBoard).

Using the course management system's private journal tool designed specifically to enable the students to develop their clinical reasoning skills for this intervention planning assignment, students and the course instructor begin to mix fact with fiction, as each student begins to construct an occupational profile of this very complex individual. This occupational profile is "a summary of information that describes [Dan's] occupational history and experiences, patterns of daily living, interests, values, and needs" (AOTA, 2008, p. 649).

The construction of Dan's occupational profile requires students to begin to use procedural, interactive, conditional, and narrative clinical rea-

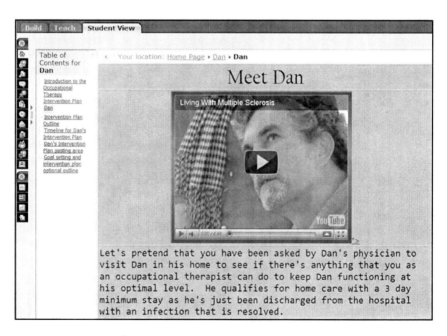

FIGURE 6.1. (Imafilmaker, 2006)

soning. They also begin to develop a plan for posing questions that they determine are necessary in order to construct an occupational therapy intervention plan such as those presented in Table 6.1. Students first identify a model of practice in this private journal space (Figure 6.2).

This occupational therapy model of practice is a thinking frame that the student will utilize throughout the process. Some examples of what the students have chosen include the Lifestyle Performance Model (Fidler, 1996), Canadian Model of Occupational Performance (Canadian Association of Occupational Therapists, 1997, 2002) and the Model of Human Occupation (Kielhofner, 2009). Once the model has been articulated by the students, they then request reports based on assessment tools that are congruent with the model of practice. Students articulate why they feel the assessment tools are appropriate to the model with requests such as, "because I would like to approach this intervention plan through the lens of the Lifestyle Performance Model, I would like to obtain a copy of Dan's occupational configuration (a log of how he spends his time in 15–30 minute segments) because I want to see how he balances his time among the four domains of that model." The instructor provides the plausible, fictional reports (such

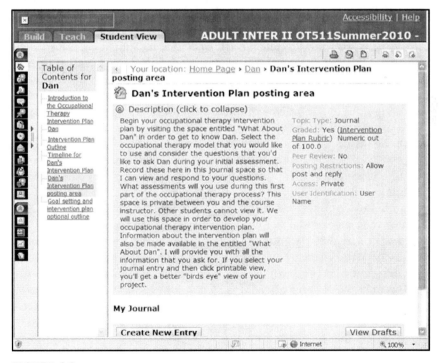

FIGURE 6.2.

as a fictitious occupational configuration) that help the student construct the occupational profile. Then the students further hone their thinking to narrow the focus of their inquiry and seek to clarify unanswered questions that they have. The course instructor responds to individual questions as Dan, and so continues the online dance or back-and-forth exchange of information that allows the students to clinically reason through the intervention planning process. Feedback from the course instructor is formative in nature, which follows best practice (Heinrich et al., 2009) in allowing the student to receive information of how their work compares to the standard. For example, the instructor can respond by posting, "That's a great choice for the Lifestyle Performance Model, and it will also help you to formulate some ideas for helping Dan make the most efficient use of his time in light of the limited endurance and fatigue that accompanies multiple sclerosis. It's a great compliment to the Lifestyle Performance Model."

If the student wants to know what Dan's living situation is like, then the instructor provides pictures of Dan's fictional home. In addition, if the student wants the results of a specific assessment tool, then the instructor provides a fictional report consistent with Dan's diagnosis and functional level. Every attempt is made to thoughtfully make the responses consistent with an individual with Dan's diagnosis and consistent with the information in the YouTube video to maintain respect for Dan and to create a realistic picture for the student. If questions or assessments are requested that are incongruent with the chosen model, or if glaring omissions are seen by the course instructor, then feedback is provided in the very early stages of the intervention planning process in order to ensure that the student experiences success as the intervention plan unfolds. In this manner, clinical reasoning skills of the individual student can be challenged and developed as the project moves along. This is consistent with best practice in teaching where the instructor takes on the role of a guide rather than "giving expert answers" (Collison, Elbaum, Haavind, & Tinker, 2000, p. 8), as is often the case in a face-to-face learning environment. This is an opportunity for the student to reflect on his or her data selection or choices, and the instructor can guide this.

After they receive the fictitious but plausible evaluation results of the instrument that they requested, students analyze and interpret the results, peeling back the layers by making a request for further evaluations in areas they determine to be necessary, such as client factors, activity demands, performance skills and patterns, as well as the context and the environment (AOTA, 2008). These may include evaluations of areas such as Dan's fatigue levels, his ability to hold and manipulate a camera, and any architectural barriers that he encounters throughout the university campus where he works. The decision about which areas need further evaluation is determined in consideration of the occupational profile that identifies those activities that hold meaning for him, the model of practice, as well as the multiple sclerosis that is part of his life. If a student omits an important component along the way, the course instructor can quickly provide the feedback so that the student can make the necessary adjustments before going too far down the wrong path. For example, a common error during this process is for the student to omit an evaluation of sensation or vision. When this happens, the instructor guides the student back to their resources that describe the clinical picture of multiple sclerosis to allow them to discover what questions they should be asking and what assessments they should be including. This immediate feedback is critical to enabling the student to develop clinical reasoning skills, and as with any new skill development, "direct feedback is the most constructive type of instruction" (Collison et al., 2000, p. 41). A student who requests evaluations for Dan and neglects to ask for a type of work or environmental evaluation will be challenged by the course instructor to think about how Dan's occupations are being impacted by the disease. In this case, the course instructor would encourage the student to go back to the YouTube video where (the real Dan) clearly articulates the passion that he has for his work as a photography professor, a passion which the student needs to understand before formulating an intervention plan that has relevance to Dan's quality of life. In this guided journey through the intervention planning process, the students learn how to organize their thoughts in this very complex process that we know as clinical reasoning. This feedback loop enables the instructor to take on a "project manager" role, rather than the provider of facts (Collison et al., 2000). In addition, the instructor is able to provide "a highly interactive succession of learning experiences that lead to the resolution of a problem" (Garrison & Vaughan, 2008, p. 25), which is considered to be best practice in the online learning environment and in this case an intervention plan results.

Once the students have gathered all of the evaluation results that are needed, they are then guided to formulate an exhaustive list of strengths and weaknesses. In collaboration with the course instructor who acts as Dan within the electronic journal, the intervention priorities are set and the students go about formulating goals. This collaboration makes this experience unique, enabled by the technology. Once measurable goals are established, the students proceed to formulate an intervention plan for how they would engage Dan to meet these goals. Specific intervention proposals are researched by the students so that they can show that they are supported by the literature. Students also provide a reflection of the experience. This "purposeful discourse to collaboratively construct, critically reflect, and confirm understanding...is referred to as cognitive presence" (Garrison & Vaughan, 2008, p. 21), and this is enhanced by the technology of the You-Tube video and online discourse. Because there is a permanent record of

Preview - Intervention Plan Rubric

Objective/Criteria	Performance Indicators			
Identify an occupational therapy model and describe how you will be viewing this particular patient/client in consideration of this model... describe the big picture . Introduce your patient/client demonstrating respect for confidentiality	(1 points) model is somewhat integrated with Dan's life with less than 3 clear examples of how the model relates to Dan's life	(3 points) model is integrated with Dan's life with at least 3 clear examples of how the model relates to Dan's life	(5 points) model is integrated with Dan's life with at least 5 clear examples of how the model relates to Dan's life	
Consider the occupational therapy assessment data	(1 points) Assessment data is not effectively integrated into the intervention plan	(5 points) Assessment data is only partially integrated into the intervention plan or only a portion of the relevant assessment data is integrated	(10 points) Assessment data is integrated into the intervention plan.	
Identify the problems that occupational therapy can have an impact upon in a numerical list format.	(1 points) problems are not effectively identified from the assessment data with key problems omitted	(5 points) problems are only partially identified from the assessment data	(10 points) problems are identified effectively from the assessment data	

FIGURE 6.3.

"logical process and hypothesized solutions [that are] rationally justified and defended," (Garrison & Vaughan, 2008, p. 23), that captures the capacity of the educational technology. This would be very difficult to replicate in a face-to-face environment where time is limited and class size may be large. Because the journal space is a private space between the course instructor and the student, a continued appraisal of the student's critical reasoning skills as an interactive experience is possible. Students who get off track can quickly be brought back to task with feedback that helps build in success for the student. This success is integral for motivating students and building their self-esteem to learn.

All along the way, the student is provided with feedback that is designed to facilitate their learning and that is clearly related to helping them gain success in meeting the assignment objectives. These objectives relate to the grading rubric which the student is introduced to at the onset (see Figures 6.3 and 6.4).

	(1 points)	(5 points)	(10 points)
Demonstrate a direct link between the research evidence and the intervention strategies that you've chosen.	there is not a link articluated	a link is not clear	a direct link has been clearly established and well developed
Discuss the discharge plans for this patient/client	(1 points) discharge plans for this patient/client are not clearly articulated AND do not appear reasonable	(3 points) discharge plans for this patient/client are not clearly articulated OR do not appear reasonable	(5 points) discharge plans for this patient/client are clearly articulated and reasonable
Discuss how the model that you chose guided the development of your intervention plan.	(1 points) discussion does not demonstrate an understanding of the model	(5 points) discussion demonstrates somewhat of an understanding of the model but is missing key elements	(10 points) discussion demonstrated a clear understanding of the model
Reflect on the intervention planning process. What was your take home message? What did you learn from this experience?	(1 points) Discussion demonstrates that the student has not reflected on this intervention planning process	(3 points) Discussion demonstrates that the student has only superficially reflected on this intervention planning process	(5 points) Discussion demonstrates that the student has reflected on this intervention planning process
spelling and grammar	(1 points) intervention plan contains 6 or more spelling or grammatical errors	(3 points) intervention plan contains 1-5 spelling or grammatical errors	(5 points) intervention plan is free from grammatical and spelling errors

out of 100

`OK`

FIGURE 6.4.

It is important that the instructor consider both the content of the feedback, as well as the feedback strategy, which should include an effective method for communicating this feedback to the student (Hatziapostolou & Paraskakis, 2010), so that students engage with the content that has been provided by the course instructor. As stated earlier, technology provides an administratively efficient method to manage multiple assignments and archives the students' work (Heinrich et al., 2009). In addition, it becomes clear the extent to which the student is able to understand and internalize the feedback that was given, an important piece to the student's learning as students don't always read or understand feedback that is provided by course instructors (Juwah et al., 2004). Reflection should be thoughtful and meet the criteria as outlined in Table 6.4. Feedback is built into this learning experience, and this reflection piece enables a student to build meaning into the experience (Garrison & Vaughan, 2008). The online environment is more conducive to this kind of reflection than a face-to-face learning environment.

As with any teaching experience, reflection on the student feedback can inform the content that needs to be further clarified or reinforced (Juwah et al., 2004) as well as the revision of the experience for future learning experiences (Heinrich et al., 2009). Although this has been done with Dan, it was done in the context of an overall course evaluation as part of a curriculum self-study. Instructor-generated feedback is only one form of feedback. Student self-reflection, or the student evaluating his or her own work, is an

TABLE 6.4. Principles of Good Feedback

SEVEN PRINCIPLES OF GOOD FEEDBACK PRACTICE
Good feedback:
1. helps clarify what good performance is (goals, criteria, expected standards);
2. facilitates the development of self-assessment (reflection) in learning;
3. delivers high quality information to students about their learning;
4. encourages teacher and peer dialogue around learning;
5. encourages positive motivational beliefs and self-esteem;
6. provides opportunities to close the gap between current and desired performance;
7. provides information to teachers that can be used to help shape the teaching.

Note: By Nicol and MacFarlane-Dick (2006), p. 7.

essential element to helping students develop into self-regulated learners (Nicol & MacFarlane-Dick, 2006). This project can be further developed with more opportunities for student self-evaluation in order to empower them as self-regulated learners.

CONCLUSION

Consistent with the self-reflection that the authors encouraged in students, they also reflected on how well the process of clinical reasoning evolved using the following questions (see Figure 6.3):

1. Are there opportunities for the student to develop skills and expertise in all levels of the clinical reasoning process (procedural, interactive, condition and narrative)? Students are introduced to information about Dan that fit into all of these components such as his age, diagnosis, profession, impact of multiple sclerosis on his photography, family life, vocational goals, and how the diagnosis is changing his life's story.
2. Does the instructor have opportunities to interact with students in a manner that facilitates their movement from novice to expert?
    a. Does the instructor mentor the clinical reasoning process? The instructor has regular contact via the online journal within the learning management system (BlackBoard).
    b. Does the instructor provide formative feedback? The instructor is able to provide feedback that the student then responds to. In this fashion, the student's thinking is guided.
    c. Is it clear that the student understands the content and nature of the feedback? By the next entry that the student makes, the

       instructor can clearly evaluate whether the student understood and has incorporated the feedback.

    d. Is there opportunity for the student to develop as independent thinkers (ie. Is there more than one "right answer" to the case?) This is encouraged and facilitated by the technology. This would not be feasible without the technology. Students choose their own model of practice, and from this choice a unique plan unfolds. As occupational therapists, we engage individuals in meaningful activities. There are many ways to accomplish this and there are many ways that this engagement impacts the lifestyle of the recipients of occupational therapy. This assignment allows for limitless possibilities for outcomes.

3.   Do students have the opportunity to reflect on their decisions? This is a requirement and is viewed as integral to a developing professional. The reflection is articulated by the student in the journal space.

4.   Do students have the opportunity to critique and evaluate themselves and their decisions? Because the feedback is formative, they know in a timely manner whether they are on the right track. They have the rubric at the outset and can monitor their progress as the learning experience unfolds.

5.   Do students meet the course objectives from the instructor's perspective? The course instructor follows this learning experience with a lab practical final examination offering a novel case study in which students apply their newly acquired clinical reasoning skills.

6.   Do students perceive that they have met the course objectives? Students have given feedback about this experience and specifically how it helps them meet the course objectives at an end of the semester course evaluation. The feedback has been very positive, with students reporting that this experience has helped them build competency.

7.   Does completion of the case move students forward in their clinical reasoning skills and provide a foundation for future practice? The generalizability of this strategy is tested during an oral final examination where students are presented with a novel case and are asked to articulate the clinical reasoning process similar to the format that they used with Dan. In this way, the effectiveness of this fictional fact methodology with Dan can be evaluated as applied to a new scenario. However, this area continues to be a challenge. We don't have good tools to date to measure clinical reasoning skills in the actual clinic. Currently the National Board Certification Examination for Occupational Therapists (NBCOT) continues to be primarily a multiple choice format. Clinical scenarios that encour-

age clinical reasoning have been incorporated into this national examination.

Dan has introduced us to the challenges of creating meaningful learning experiences for occupational therapy students. While the technology that allows this type of dynamic learning environment is being outpaced by the research, the interactive approach that is enabled by the technology illustrates how authentically this learning environment can be constructed. This project with Dan builds on the literature that supports best practices in clinical reasoning, distance education, and occupational therapy.

REFERENCES

American Occupational Therapy Association. (2007). Accreditation standards for a master's-degree-level educational program for the occupational therapist. *American Journal of Occupational Therapy, 61,* 652–661.

American Occupational Therapy Association. (2008). Occupational therapy practice framework: Domain and process (2nd ed.). *American Journal of Occupational Therapy, 62,* 625–683.

Amini, D. (2010). Defining the term occupation. *OT Practice, 15*(17), 6.

Baum, C. (2007) Philosophy of occupational therapy education. *American Journal of Occupational Therapy, 61*(6), 678.

Bruer, J. (1993). The mind's journey from novice to expert: If we know the route, we can help students negotiate their way. *American Educator, 17(2), 6–15, 38–46.*

Canadian Association of Occupational Therapists. (1997, 2002). *Enabling occupation: An occupational therapy perspective.* Ottawa, ON: CAOT Publications ACE.

Case-Smith, J. (2009). *Occupational therapy for children* (6th ed.). Baltimore, MD: Mosby.

Collins, A, Brown, J., & Holm, A. (1991). Cognitive apprenticeship: Making thinking visible. *American Educator, 15(3), 6–11, 36–46.*

Collison, G., Elbaum, B., Haavind, S., & Tinker, R. (2000). *Facilitating online learning: Effective strategies for moderators.* Madison, WI: Atwood Publishing.

Fidler, G. S. (1996). Life-Style performance: From profile to conceptual model. *American Journal of Occupational Therapy, 50,* 139–147.

Fidler, G. S. (2003). What is the question? *Occupational Therapy Journal of Research, 23*(3), 86–87.

Garrison, D.R., & Vaughan, N. (2008). *Blended learning in higher education: Framework, principles, and guidelines.* San Francisco, CA: Jossey-Bass.

Hammel, J., Royeen, C., Bagatell, N., Jensen, G., Loveland, J., & Stone, G. (1999). Student perspectives on problem-based learning in an occupational therapy curriculum: A multiyear qualitative evaluation. *American Journal of Occupational Therapy, 53*(2), 199–206.

Hatziapostolou, T., & Paraskakis, I. (2010). Enhancing the impact of formative feedback on student learning through an online feedback system. *Electronic Journal of e-Learning, 8,* 111–122. Retrieved from: www.ejel.org

Heinrich, E., Milne, J., & Moore, M. (2009). An investigation into E-Tool use for formative assignment assessment—Status and recommendations. *Educational Technology & Society, 12*(4), 176–192. Retrieved from: http://www.ifets.info/journals/12_4/16.pdf

Hinojosa, J. (2007) Becoming innovators in an era of hyperchange. [Eleanor Clarke Slagle Lecture] *American Journal of Occupational Therapy, 61*(6), 629–637.

Imafilmaker (Creator). (2006, May 17). *Living with Multiple Sclerosis* [Video] Retrieved from http://www.youtube.com/user/Imafilmmaker#p/u/2/TNPQF-Wk8fqs.

Juwah, C., Macfarlane-Dick, D., Matthew, B., Nicol, D., & Smith, B. (2004) The Higher Education Academy. *Enhancing student learning through effective formative feedback.* [Online]. http://www.heacademy.ac.uk/assets/York/documents/resources/resourcedatabase/id353_senlef_guide.pdf

Kielhofner, G. (2009). *Conceptual foundations of occupational therapy* (3rd ed.). Philadelphia, PA: F.A. Davis.

Lave, J., & Wenger, E. (1991). *Situated learning: Legitimate peripheral participation.* New York, NY: Cambridge University Press.

Lysaght, R., & Bent, M. (2005). A comparative analysis of case presentation modalities used in clinical reasoning coursework in occupational therapy. *American Journal of Occupational Therapy, 59*(3), 314–324.

Mattingly, C. & Fleming, M. (1994). *Clinical reasoning: Forms of inquiry in a therapeutic practice.* Philadelphia, PA: FA Davis.

Neistadt, M. (1999). Teaching clinical reasoning as a thinking frame. *American Journal of Occupational Therapy, 52*(3), 221–229.

Neistadt, M., Wright, J., & Mulligan, S. (1998). Clinical reasoning case studies as teaching tools. *American Journal of Occupational Therapy, 52,* 125–132.

Neistadt, M., & Smith, R. (1997). Teaching diagnostic reasoning using a classroom-as-clinic methodology with videotapes. *American Journal of Occupational Therapy, 49*(4), 349–353.

Nicol, D.J., & MacFarlane-Dick, D. (2006). Formative assessment and self-regulated learning: A model and seven principles of good feedback practice. *Studies in Higher Education, 31,* 199–218. Retrieved from http://www.reap.ac.uk/public/Papers/DN_SHE_Final.pdf

Pendelton, H., & Schultz-Krohn, W. (2010). *Occupational therapy practice skills for physical dysfunction* (6th ed.). Baltimore, MD: Mosby.

Resnick, L. (1987). *Education and learning to think.* Washington, DC: National Academy Press.

Scaffa, M., & Wooster, D. (2004). Effects of problem based learning on clinical reasoning in occupational therapy. *American Journal of Occupational Therapy, 58*(3), 333–336.

Schell, B. (2009). Professional reasoning in practice. In E. Crepeau, E. Cohn, & B. Schell (Eds.), *Willard & Spackman's occupational therapy* (11th ed,. pp. 314–327). Philadelphia: Lippincott.

Trombly, C., & Radomski, M. (2008). *Occupational therapy for physical dysfunction* (6th ed.). Philadelphia, PA: Lippincott, Williams & Wilkins.

VanLeit, B. (1995). Using the case method to develop clinical reasoning skills in problem-based learning. *American Journal of Occupational Therapy, 49(4), 349–353.*

Vroman, K., & MacRae, N. (1999). How should the effectiveness of problem-based learning in occupational therapy education be examined? *American Journal of Occupational Therapy, 53*(5), 533–536.

West, C., Farmer, J., & Wolff P. (1991). *Instructional design: Implications from cognitive science.* Boston: Ally and Bacon.

Yerxa, E. (1992). Some implications of occupational therapy history for its epistemology, values and relation to medicine. *American Journal of Occupational Therapy, 46*(1), 79–83.

UNIT 4

BEYOND THE CLASSROOM

CHAPTER 7

UTILIZING SOCIAL MEDIA FOR DEMOCRATIC SERVICE-LEARNING PRACTICE

A Framework and Guide for Educators

**Cara R. Lynch, Elizabeth E. Henry,
Lisa V. Bardwell, and Jennifer A. Richter**

At its best, service-learning is problem-based learning with young people focused on addressing real issues in their community. When coupled with an effective use of social media, we have a mechanism for instigating civic action, and housing record of it, thus expanding democratic space and youth action in our physical and virtual environments. By combining high-quality service-learning with critical use of social media, young people can have participatory learning opportunities that allow them to shape their experience in both their local and virtual communities. The combination allows young people to relate to their communities as civic actors who understand that social media is shaped by its users, and that democracy and community are "always in the making," dependent upon the acts of the populace (Benson, Harkavy, & Pucket, 2007; Greene, 1995). This chapter explores the Earth Force Process, as an exemplar of service-learning, and social media's applicability to it. When brought into a service-learning context, social media can form a foundation

Designing Problem-Driven Instruction with Online Social Media, pages 127–146
Copyright © 2012 by Information Age Publishing

for educators to tap into the culture of youth, provide an opportunity for youth to develop critical use of information and social media, and equip them with essential skills needed to address issues in their communities.{\abs}

INTRODUCTION

"Our problem is not that we don't have enough information. I mean, if there are children starving in Somalia, it is not because we don't have enough information. If crime is rampant on the streets of New York or Boston, it's not because people don't have enough information. Think of any serious problem today and I think you'll have to conclude it has nothing to do with insufficient information."

— *Neil Postman (2004, p. 6)*

At the turn of the 21st century, journalists and politicians documented the fraying of America's civic fabric, noting the lack of involvement Americans had in our social institutions, a lack of belief in the democratic ideals of America, and an overall sense of political misdirection (Putnam, 1995; Swartz, Campbell, & Pestana, 2009). Media ecologist Neil Postman (2004) termed this a lack of a transcendent narrative, or a missing sense of moral guidance and social purpose normally needed to organize and make sense of our experiences. How we interface with media as a result of the world wide web and newer media technologies of late 20th century accounts in part for these observed downturns in civic participation (Postman, 2004; Putnam, 1995). In part, it is because many people lack an "organizing principle" of what to do with information to transform it into something useful, something to positively benefit others or the common good. In part, it is because we are unpracticed in habits of everyday democracy (Lewis, 2008).

Certain civic trends suggest that this might be shifting. In particular, the involvement and interest our young people have in their communities continues to show upward trends (Corporation for National and Community Service, 2010). This current generation of young people spends more time volunteering in communities than we have seen in over 50 years (Corporation for National and Community Service, 2010). What has also shifted are newer forms of internet communication, primarily mediated by Web 2.0 social media platforms, which allow for more opportunities for the common person to exchange, collaborate on, and publish information. Predictably, this generation of youth spends a considerable amount of its free time online interfacing through social networking sites such as Facebook, Myspace, and Twitter (Pryor, Hurtado, DeAngelo, Palucki-Blake, & Tran, 2009).

This combination of youth involvement in communities and in social media has prompted researchers and practitioners of service-learning to ask how we might use online experiences and socializing to motivate and support youth to take action on real issues in their communities (Lewis & Richardson, 2008). In this chapter, we overlay that with the question of *how do we transcribe real-world action back into meaningful Web 2.0 interaction?* We contend that seeing service-learning and social media as complimentary learning tools can help young people become critical actors and contributors in both our physical and online communities.

By connecting students to their environments and communities, and then using social media for research and communication related to their service-learning projects, students learn about changing their local environment and how to shape and use social media for civic purpose and expression. Service-learning, and the Earth Force process in particular, is one practical method of combining the civic inclinations of young people with their interest in social media. This chapter explores how the educator can integrate social media into his or her service-learning practice using the Earth Force process. It furthermore explores why educators and young people would employ social media alongside this process.

Why Social Media? Why Service-Learning? Why Now?

Similar to the motivations that drive service-learning practitioners and students, the creation of Web 2.0 platforms arose from programmers' desires to support public dialogue, collaborative debate, and artistic creation to open up a new democratic space for expression of ideas. Reflecting on the ideals of Web 2.0 platforms, Anderson (2007) writes

> In short, these are ideas about building something more than a global information space; something with much more of a social angle to it. Collaboration, contribution and community are the order of the day and there is a sense in which some think that a new "social fabric" is being constructed before our eyes. (p. 14)

As an active, problem-based learning strategy, service-learning cultivates a similar ethic of practice. It drives teachers, students, and community partners to focus on how communities can be changed for the better.

Ten years into the 21st century, we see an impressive array of communication tools, such as texting, blogging, tagging, wikis, email, Facebook, and Twitter, playing a central role in the lives of young people. Nearly 86% of college students use social networking sites as a regular form of communication (Lewis and Richardson, 2008). Facebook (2011) reports that of its hundreds of millions of users, most are high school or college-aged youth and young adults. What would it look like to gather this obsession with social media within the context of the classroom? How can teachers, students, and community partners use these media to make the classroom a literacy and media rich environment, so that students are engaged and the learning is relevant?

The National Service-Learning Clearinghouse (2010) defines service-learning as "a teaching and learning strategy that integrates meaningful community service with instruction and reflection to enrich the learning experience, teach civic responsibility, and strengthen communities" (n.p.). The benefits of high quality service-learning include preparing students with 21st century skills, increasing student motivation and engagement in school and their learning, enhancing civic and social skills; increasing academic achievement; and improving community involvement at schools (Billig, 2004; Furco & Root, 2010; Keilsmeier, 2010; Melchior, 2009).

With roots extending back to the pragmatic theories of Dewey and the critical theories of Freire, service-learning as a practice makes it the responsibility of the educator to use students' physical and social realities as the grounds for meaningful learning (Dewey, 1938; Freire & Macedo, 1987; Keilsmeier, 2010). Adept practitioners of service-learning will find that social media complements their students' problem-based learning experience, and is actually a necessary learning tool present in the student's social, political, and economic realities.

Through combining social media with instruction and reflection related to the service-learning process, educators and students learn to use multiple modalities of communication structured around the civic enrichment of our communities. Moreover, the integration of social media into this practice legitimizes youth culture; provides rich interdisciplinary opportunities for youth to gather, organize, and use relevant information; and reinforces youth civic engagement opportunities.

Social Media Legitimizes Youth Culture

Young people are familiar with social media and use it regularly. Thompson (2009) notes that thirty-eight percent of the writing a student does in a day is "life writing," or informal correspondence through texting, emailing, or posting on Facebook. Given our students' familiarity with this medium, to ignore it is akin to dismissing the backgrounds and communities that help define who young people are and what they know. Moreover, it discounts skills they are already cultivating and which are relevant to the needs of the classroom.

While there are challenges with introducing social media into the learning environment, using these media could doubly benefit our students. First of all, the platforms are familiar to many of them and can reinforce prior knowledge and skills. Secondly, social media are tools we can use to move students towards deeper levels of understanding, and in certain cases, into networks of supportive learning environments customized to help them ask questions and pursue interests that arise from their observations of what their community needs.

Students are apt to learn better when they have an interest in a topic, and when their teachers can tap into their culture to provide them a relevant, critical, and intellectually challenging opportunity to examine what influences their culture. Providing opportunities for students to examine and address issues relevant to their school, community, and physical environment helps them become civic actors and change agents. Social media provide just one mode of taking a familiar experience and turning it into a learning scenario. Connecting an experience of the critical analysis of social media to problem-based service-learning multiplies the learning opportunities that begin from what Vygotsky (1978) termed students' *zones of proximal learning.*

Integrating youth popular culture into the classroom as a teaching tool provides both an opportunity to connect with youth around what they know and are immersed in and an opportunity to teach critical inquiry of it. In this regard, it becomes a rich teaching text and an act of equity (Duncan-Andrade, 2004). It legitimizes the students' culture and allows them to examine its shortcomings and strengths. Through that examination, they begin to make popular culture explicit. That act empowers their choices around consumption of popular culture and, thus, alternatives for creating their culture.

Service-learning that is grounded within a local community achieves this very same purpose. It takes what students know about their surrounding environments and communities and transforms it into a text they can examine and revise. In this way students become responsive to the realities of their surroundings and responsible for their interactions there. Likewise, when an educator brings social media into the classroom within the context of service-learning, students expand their understanding of its use as they explore it as a community-based space of expression. In one regard, social media is used as an element of youth popular culture, and in another it is utilized as a malleable format where youth can shape and express their culture through it.

Enriching How Students Find, Use, and Share Information

Young people need to know how to access and make sense of more information than ever before, especially when it comes to environmental and social issues. Researchers acknowledge that complex environmental issues interface with some of our most pressing social issues and political injustices (Advisory Committee for Environmental Research and Education, 2009). In its report on skills needed of the 21st century student, the New Commission on the Skills of the American Workforce (2006) outlined multiple skills students need in order to properly contribute to the changing world economy. At the top of the list is that students must know how to solve real-world problems, and that in order to do so, they must know how to make interdisciplinary connections and how to synthesize data and information from multiple sources. Both reports focus on the interconnected reality of our global economy, and thus the need for students to be able to communicate with and appreciate diverse cultures. They further acknowledge the role that newer technologies, such as immersive virtual environments and social media, are playing in cultivating these problem-based learning skills of the 21st century student.

High-quality service-learning provides a framework for young people to explore and make sense of their local environment by mediating how they gather and use information (Bardwell & Kaplan, 2008). Most service-learning begins with an information-gathering step, when students start learning about the world around them and problems they might address. The Earth Force Six Step Process is a model grounded in the local community and environment where students go to school or where they reside. It is one method designed to encourage student engagement and interaction with their community, its members, and, thus, their local civic agencies. During the first phase of this process, students may conduct interviews, collect hard data, and find original sources.

Service-learning is inherently interdisciplinary, particularly if the educator carefully structures opportunities for gathering and analyzing important physical, historical, and cultural data related to the issues students choose to address. Similarly, service-learning makes it possible for an educator to organize a thoughtful alignment of various information environments, which reinforce students' abilities to pick out patterns, assess options for actions, and synthesize information from diverse perspectives. Their familiar surroundings and modes of communication become rich learning resources that provide feedback and coherency. For example, using the Earth Force process, students focus on their local community, articulating what they see as issues there and organizing their information gathering to address those issues. As they move through the service-learning process, students synthesize their research and findings in order to develop a project they think will address their chosen issue. They are responsible for identifying stakeholders and justifying to them why their issue is important. This process is similar to how one parses out arguments and develops and organizes an essay. In this sense, hard data, social experience in one's environment, and key aspects of literacy all contribute to a holistic and relevant learning opportunity tied to changing one's community.

This is a different age of research, and given the sheer volume of constantly changing and updated information on the web, our students need those resources to adapt to the changing media environment. They furthermore need them to reinforce traditional literacy skills. When done skillfully, an educator can structure the experience so that it enriches literacy, providing explicit opportunities to link this learning process to skills of parsing out arguments, developing, and organizing an essay or research paper. By intentionally linking the service-learning process to social media, educators can quickly connect students to data stored online and to specialists who know about the specific issues that students have identified in their community through service-learning. They also provide outlets for students to publicly share their knowledge, an act that in its own right, allows students to shape the virtual environment, connecting others to issues important to them. Educators could use this as an opportunity for students to write a persuasive essay, and then develop it into an animated cartoon to be shared on Teachertube, the school's internal news network, or the local newspaper's blogging site. In this sense, hard data, social experience in one's environment, and key aspects of literacy all contribute to a holistic and relevant learning opportunity tied to changing one's community. The multiple environments where our students spend their time can be woven together to support the development of research, analysis, writing, and civic skills.

Reinforcing Strong Ties for Community Action

Service-learning is about real work in our communities, work meant to strengthen the civic integrity of our common lives. Creative, civic work as Harry Boyte (2001) might say is bringing diverse people together around issues important to the community. Used apart from real, civic action, Web 2.0 cannot provide the kind of mobilized muscle we need to effectively address the serious issues facing us in the 21st century. It can, however, serve as an outlet for public voice and be a strategic way to build group motivation such that people take to the streets or grab their shovels and buckets for a clean-up.

In "Small Change: Why the Revolution Will not be Tweeted," Malcolm Gladwell (2010) comments on the necessary components of civic action. He writes,

> But there is something else at work here, in the outsized enthusiasm for social media. Fifty years after one of the most extraordinary episodes of social upheaval in American history, we seem to have forgotten what activism is.... The kind of activism associated with social media isn't like this at all. The platforms of social media are built around weak ties. (p. 2)

He is referring to the difference between broad networks of people gathering around a cause, such as the recent protest in Tehran attributed to Facebook and Twitter, and those of organizations and movements that had people organizing through "strong ties" of face-to-face relationship and commitment.

Gladwell (2010) presents a critique relevant to the classroom. As he questions what constitutes activism, the educator questions what constitutes meaningful learning. When does learning, like activism, truly influence one's surroundings? Are actions in cyber space enough? Is de-contextualized literacy relevant to student learning? Combing service-learning with social media provides an opportunity for educators to engage students as agents of change, within their communities and among individuals with "strong ties" to their issues. At the same time, it also creates an opportunity for practitioners and groups to find research and share projects and setbacks within supportive social media networks.

This is much like the reality social media is playing across the globe as more groups continue to find support and motivation to convene for political action (Brandzel, 2010). Social media can support the work of our youth and community members by serving as another venue where they can convene as a local civic network. Community members can learn about the progress of the students' work, and also share a deliberative space with youth. The rest of the community can see what its youth are doing and how they are invested in the future of their community. The groups of youth and adults learn from one another to gather and maintain support to carry forward the real, physical work and change needed in a living democracy.

THE EARTH FORCE PROCESS AND SOCIAL MEDIA

Multiple versions of the service-learning process exist, such as the National Youth Leadership Council (NYLC) service-learning cycle, Public Achievement, PeaceJam, and Earth Force. We center our discussion on the Earth Force six-step process because it is a school-based, curricular strategy that focuses explicitly on students taking civic action within their schools and communities. A distinctive quality of the Earth Force process is that young people become involved in a larger political process of effecting longer-term systemic change in their communities. Students design projects to change policy or practice rather than providing a charity model of service. The essence of this process (see Figure 7.1) is that through exploring a local, physical environment—oftentimes a school building, schoolyard, or neighborhood—students identify an issue and go through a process of learning and democratic consensus about how to address it by designing and implementing a project aimed at addressing its root causes.

The description of the Earth Force process below provides working definitions of each step of the Earth Force process. A discussion of social media's applicability to high-quality service-learning follows. Both are meant to provide the educator with a practical guide to enrich her or his service-learning practice with social media. Please see the Appendix for suggested examples of social media tools that can support the learning of students as they move through each step.

FIGURE 7.1.   The Earth Force process is depicted as a sequence of learning. As students move from one step to the next, they delve deeper into understanding root causes of issues. This formal and non-formal approach to researching community issues allows for students to collect and analyze data from a variety of sources. Through their research, students might want to revisit a previous learning step in the process in order to better understand the issue or the choices they made. It is a sequenced framework that allows for students to continually inform their decisions as they take public action.

The Launch

The launch is the step that lays the foundation for a successful Earth Force process. As a precursor to the community environmental inventory, this step provides an opportunity for students to explore the concepts of community, inviting dialogue about civic roles and environmental citizenship. This step prepares students with a map of the process they will use to solve a local problem and constructive opportunities to define their role within their communities and schools.

Step 1: Community Inventory

Youth and educators define the community for their service-learning project—possibly their school, an area of their neighborhood near the school, part of their watershed, or their city. Once they have established community boundaries, they use various methods of taking an inventory of all of the strengths and issues within their community. This may include observations, environmental audits, surveys, or interviews with community members.

For example, a sixth grade group spent time in their local park and a nearby river, observing patterns of human behavior and noting any issues they saw. They also talked with local business owners about changes in the neighborhood over the years and conducted water quality testing with an environmental education center.

Step 2: Issue Selection

The second step introduces a very powerful skill—criteria-based decision making. With the list of issues in hand, young people learn to use criteria to decide which issue to work on.

After using different inventory methods, students in our example identified litter in the park, electronics waste in the river, and lack of youth programming at the recreation center as the most important issues to them. Based on criteria that included their own level of interest, access to resources for research, and relevance to their school community, students used criteria-based decision making to choose the dumping of electronics waste as the issue they would address.

Step 3: Policy and Practice Research

The group uses this step to determine what else it needs to know about the issue and develops a strategy for gathering that information, just as the group did for the inventory. This might include going on field trips, inviting guest speakers, or developing surveys. It is important that students access perspectives that represent all sides of an issue in their research. They learn the difference between policies and practices, and reach out to stakeholders. The educator encourages them to think about people affected by the issue, those causing it, those who might impact policies related to the issue, or those who have done something to address a similar issue in their own community or in others.

Returning to our sixth graders, they worked with environmental organizations to learn about the impact of electronics waste in rivers and streams. After taking photos of the problem areas, they talked with local recycling agencies to research options for proper disposal of electronics and with their city's waste management department to learn whether there were policies in place about disposal of hazardous materials. In addition, they surveyed community residents to ask how they dispose of various materials and gauge their understanding of the impact of improper disposal.

Step 4: Strategy Selection

In the fourth step, students create a goal statement to envision the change they would like to see, and they brainstorm possible strategies for getting there. They then return to criteria-based decision making, this time using all of their research to inform a strategy for change.

After learning that there is no standard procedure for disposing of electronic waste, students identified a few strategies that might impact this issue—start a community-wide electronics recycling day, propose curbside recycling to the city, or have a community cleanup of the riverbank. Using criteria, the group ultimately decided that the most sustainable change would come from a curbside program, so making a proposal to city council would be the best strategy to implement.

Step 5: Taking Action

This step involves creating and implementing an action plan and can also include developing a plan with a timeline, budget, and roles for each member of the group.

Our sixth grade class compiled all of the data it had collected from its own research and work with partners and contacted the city to set up a time to present. The students invited some of their partners to attend the presentation. The city had not realized that the stream was being used as a dumping ground for electronics. Acknowledging that there are insufficient means for proper disposal within the city, officials agreed to work with the students to include them in planning for curbside recycling of electronics, with the hope of instituting the service within two years.

Step 6: Looking Back and Ahead

While reflection is integral to each step of the process, this final, structured reflection step is a look back at the whole process. It may include a celebration and time for students to share what they have done with a larger community. The reflection process helps students value what they have learned and accomplished and think about what they might do differently next time.

The students participating in the electronics recycling project learned how they could get essential information from adults about their issue and how to use research to validate ideas for community change. Part of their reflection process included determining how some students would stay connected with Waste Management to ensure their voices were heard as a plan for curbside recycling developed.

SOCIAL MEDIA OUTLETS FOR SERVICE-LEARNING

The National Youth Leadership Council (NYLC), PeaceJam, Earth Force, and other service-learning providers continue to develop new tools to connect educators to one another. For example, NYLC hosts webinars through its Generator School Network; PeaceJam has a live chat and blogging space on its website; and Earth Force serves as an intermediary for educators and students to interact and build supportive relationships on Facebook. After researching which social media tools fit one's teaching purposes, students and educators can determine the appropriate use of social media in their service-learning project. Social media tools can complement each step of the service-learning process, as well as elements of high-quality service-learning projects. In order to know where to begin, we will describe some of the most common social media outlets and provide insight into the purpose of each.

A blog, or web log, is way to share information where content is uploaded and visitors who read the information may have an opportunity to comment on the posts. Blogs have become a popular way for individuals to share expertise. While the idea of creating a cyberspace discussion forum for young people can be intimidating, there are sites that have created social media tools to meet the needs of the education community. Providers such as Edublogs.org and Kidblog.com allow users to create free accounts that have manageable privacy controls for the moderator and are typically not blocked by school and district firewalls (Kessler, 2010). Blogs can provide a great platform for students and educators to share progress on service-learning projects, insight into their own research, pose discussion topics related to the issue being addressed, or even to track the work they are doing outside of the classroom. Most blog sites have the capacity to support uploading photos, podcasts, and videos to make the interactions even more dynamic.

Twitter provides a venue for building virtual partnerships and figuring out who might be a potential stakeholder in addressing issues. Twitter is considered the most popular microblogging site, which the United States government defines as sharing information in the form of a status update that is best used when it leads to two-way conversations with others (Levy, 2010). Using the Twitter search function to look for keywords associated with an issue will produce the most recent messages by other users talking about the same topic. Many users, in addition to sharing status updates, will post links to articles and other resources that can be very valuable in researching issues. It will be one of the best sources for finding out what people have tried in other communities to address similar issues. Having a sense for what others have done can often facilitate students coming up with ways of addressing an issue. Either learning from the mistakes of others or finding valuable insight into creative solutions can inform how students choose to approach solving their own issue. The microblogging conversations are infinitely more powerful when used as a way of engaging people in a conversation, versus just reading others' posts or sharing one's own updates. Commenting on others' posts, asking questions, and otherwise engaging in conversation leads to a much more meaningful engagement and relationship building, thereby getting more attention to what the students are doing to research and address their issue.

Facebook has notably become an enormously powerful social media platform. With more than 500 million active users, it is adding individual users at a rapid rate (Facebook, 2011). Facebook allows users to connect with other individuals and organizations through personal friend requests and fan pages. Fan pages are easy to create and allow the administrator to gain support for issues, causes, or products. While it may be appropriate for some service-learning groups to create a fan page to promote their project, there seems to be a never-ending debate about whether it is appropriate for students and educators to interact on Facebook. If district or state standards deem a fan page appropriate, students can post updates on what they are doing with their projects, pose questions to those following the project, and share video clips or photos. For other groups, it may be more effective for facilitators and students alike to share service-learning updates with their own personal networks and offer ways that their friends and family can get involved and support the work.

When it comes to sharing stories, nothing is more powerful than seeing youth in action. YouTube, Vimeo and other video sharing sites can allow for detailed updates and visuals of progress, interviews with stakeholders, or student reflections. TeacherTube (www.teachertube.com), like EduBlogs, is a site that permits only education-related posts by its users, thereby creating a safer and more accessible way for students to share video clips. They can also search by topic or keyword on any of the video sharing sites to see what information others are sharing as part of their research.

Social bookmarking sites, such as De.li.cious (www.delicious.com) or StumbleUpon (www.stumbleupon.com), can store resources students want to use in their research. Social bookmarking sites allow users to bookmark web sites of interest and tag them with keywords, thereby making them easy to search. Users can also search sites saved by others. In terms of finding articles and other relevant research sites, social bookmarking helps students keep track of and categorize their resources, as well as find articles others are using.

There are many opportunities to integrate social media into any service-learning process. The choices are overwhelming. It is important that students and educators alike work within guidelines and parameters that may be set by districts or administrators when beginning to use social media tools. Starting small, with one tool at a time, keeps the exploration manageable.

HIGH QUALITY SERVICE-LEARNING STANDARDS AND SOCIAL MEDIA

The eight service-learning standards for quality practice set forth by the National Youth Leadership Council (NYLC) in 1998 and adopted by most major service-learning organizations, including Earth Force, give criteria for ensuring that the work students are doing to address local issues has a lasting impact on the youth and their communities. Figure 7.2 includes the standards of high quality service-learning and their definitions. While social media can align well with any of them, we will examine more carefully reflection, diversity, partnerships and addressing a real community need as they relate to opportunities within social media.

Reflection

Step 6 of the Earth Force Process: Looking Back and Ahead, encourages process reflection, but it is worth repeating that reflection should be hap-

- *Meaningful service* - Service-learning actively engages participants in meaningful and personally relevant service activities.
- *Link to the curriculum* – Service-learning is intentionally used as an instructional strategy to meet learning goals and/or content standards.
- *Reflection* - Service-learning incorporates multiple challenging reflection activities that are ongoing and that prompt deep thinking and analysis about oneself and one's relationship to society.
- *Diversity* - Service-learning promotes understanding of diversity and mutual respect among all participants.
- *Youth Voice* - Service-learning provides youth with a strong voice in planning, implementing, and evaluating service-learning experiences with guidance from adults.
- *Partnerships* - Service-learning partnerships are collaborative, mutually beneficial, and address community needs.
- *Progress monitoring* - Service-learning engages participants in an ongoing process to assess the quality of implementation and progress toward meeting specified goals, and uses results for improvement and sustainability.
- *Duration and intensity* - Service-learning has sufficient duration and intensity to address community needs and meet specified outcomes (NYLC, 2007).

FIGURE 7.2. Includes the standards of high quality service-learning and their definition. Taken from the work of the National Youth Leadership Council (2007), these standards represent the characteristics of a high-quality service-learning experience.

pening throughout the entire service-learning experience. Research indicates that frequent and varied reflection meaningfully connects students to the project in which they are engaged (RMC Research Corporation, 2007). Social media platforms are part of a larger selection of tools from which students can choose at any point in their service-learning process.

Making social media a part of the service-learning practice takes reflection to an interactive level. Blogs and wikis, for example, can house comments and discussion threads, giving the audience a chance to read and respond to the reflections. Responses validate students' thoughts and encourage students to return to their reflection, reread, expand or revise. This process moves them through analysis, evaluation and creation in the higher order thinking skills defined by the revised Bloom's taxonomy (Forehand, 2005).

Diversity

The National Youth Leadership Council (2007) introduces the importance of diversity in service-learning, "Within service-learning activities, it is particularly important to actively seek to understand and value the backgrounds and perspectives of those offering and receiving service, and to recognize and overcome stereotypes." In fact, diversity is a crucial part of any service-learning project. In terms of perspective, it is important that students research all sides of an issue they are trying to address. Teachers will want to incorporate diverse types of inventories in Step 1: The Community Inventory. During Step 2: Issue Selection, teachers and students will develop criteria that reference the high quality standards. In Step 3: Policy and Practice Research, students should engage with as wide and diverse a group of stakeholders as is reasonable, and gather accurate information through multiple research methods.

Using social media tools to seek diverse perspectives on a topic is not intended as a substitute for face-to-face interactions. They should complement the local perspectives students are gathering. However, they can help students gauge how others have addressed similar issues. Tools such as Twitter, YouTube, and blogs can provide comparisons of how issues have been addressed elsewhere, and thus connect students across communities, communicating about certain topics. This interactivity invites students to think about differences in those communities and various social and environmental factors contributing to causes of the issue. In this way, social media are again valuable tools in reaching beyond the walls of the school or the boundaries of the community.

Partnerships

The quality of a service-learning experience could likely correlate with whether it is part of a larger network of people, businesses, organizations, and others who are invested in young people discovering their natural leadership skills and ability to effect change in their communities. In the Earth Force process, partners can provide insight during Step 1: The Community Inventory by serving as resources. When engaged in Step 3: Policy and Practice Research, local partners can provide specific knowledge of policies and practices in relationship to local customs and history. During Step 5: Taking Action, partners invest time and energy working with young people as they carry out their action plan. Step 6 works here too—the reflection period is also a chance to share a permanent log with the community, especially for future reference, since many projects may become part of the natural landscape or so ingrained in the community that people forget their origins. Keeping blogs or virtual newspaper clippings is a good reference source for new practitioners. It is a way of archiving progress and ideas for improvement for successive groups of students, educators, and community partners. From allowing for frequent conversation to expanding the number of people connected, the use of social media can enhance all of the qualities of successful service-learning partnerships—commitment to a common vision, frequent and open communication, and involvement of diverse community members who work at all levels within a municipality.

Meaningful Service

The National Youth Leadership Council refers to The Alliance for Service-Learning in Education Reform's definition of 'meaningful contribution," which is, "one that fills a recognized need in the community, is appropriate to the age of the students involved, results in a tangible or visible outcome or product, and demonstrates learning outcomes" (Billig & Fredericks, 2008, n.p.). Qualities of meaningful service include a direct interaction with the community served, activities which hold students' interest, and the ability for students to see its relevance to their lives. Facilitating an opportunity during Step 1: The Community Inventory, for students to explore their own community on a virtual platform, is an easy way to encourage them to guide their own learning. Step 6: Looking Back and Ahead allows students to process the impact they had in their community, as well as the value of engaging in long-term civic action. Students can reflect on their process in public through video or podcasting. They could even engage in a virtual forum moderated by a service-learning agency.

CONCLUSION

Earth Force and other service-learning providers are learning from each other and others in the field when it comes to social media and engaging audiences online. As online technology develops, so do the opportunities to bring those tools into the classroom. Project-based learning and service-learning, in particular, are ideal instructional strategies for connecting youth with real-world experiences. Taking them to the virtual platforms adds yet another dimension to the academic and social growth of the 21st-century students.

Social media's role in service-learning is an indispensible learning tool. It offers a powerful opportunity for educators and their students to change how they engage in their community and learning. From providing multiple ways to conduct research and share information to connecting with various community partners, social media can link the classroom with the real action taking place in the community. Most importantly, the combination of service-learning and social media can help students find new democratic space in both their physical and virtual environments, one that legitimizes and values their youth culture, vision and hope for the future.

REFERENCES

Advisory Committee for Environmental Research and Education. (2009). *Transitions and tipping points in complex environmental systems.* A Report by the NSF Advisory Committee for Environmental Research and Education. Retrieved from http://www.nsf.gov/geo/ere/ereweb/ac-ere/nsf6895_ere_report_090809.pdf

Anderson, P. (2007). What is web 2.0? Ideas, technologies and implications for education. *JISC Technology and Standards Watch.* Retrieved from http://www.jisc.ac.uk/media/documents/techwatch/tsw0701b.pdf

Bardwell, L.V., & Kaplan, S. (2008). Creating a generation of problem solvers: A cognitive perspective on service-learning, *Information for Action: A Journal for Service-Learning Research with Children and Youth, 1*(1). Retrieved from http://www.servicelearningpartnership.org/ifa_journal/winter2008/CreatingaGeneration ProblemSolvers.pdf

Benson, L., Harkavy, I., & Puckett, J. (2007). *Dewey's dream: Universities and democracies in an age of education reform.* Philadelphia, PA: Temple University Press.

Billig, S., & Fredericks, L. (2008). *Meaningful service.* Retrieved from http://service-learning.org/filemanager/download/8311_meaningful_service.pdf

Billig, S. (2004). Heads, hearts, and hands: The research on K–12 service-learning. In J. Kielsmeier, M. Neal, & M. McKinnon (Eds.), *Growing to greatness* (pp. 12–25). Retrieved from http://www.nylc.org/inaction_init.cfm?oid=3698

Boyte, H. (2001). A tale of two playgrounds: Young people and politics. *American Political Science Association,* September 1, 2001. Retrieved from http://www.augsburg.edu/cdc/publicachievement/pdf/A%20tale%20of%20two%20playgrounds.pdf

Brandzel, B. (2010). What Malcolm Gladwell missed about online organizing and creating big change. *The Nation.* Retrieved from http://www.thenation.com/article/156447/what-malcolm-gladwell-missed-about-online-organizing-and-creating-big-change, Nov. 15, 2010.

Corporation for National and Community Service. (2010). *Volunteering in America: Information on volunteering and civic engagement.* Retrieved from http://www. volunteeringinamerica.gov/special/Millennials-%28born-1982-or-after%29

Dewey, J. (1938). *Experience and education.* New York, NY: Touchstone.

Duncan-Andrade, J. (2004). Your best friend or your worst enemy: Youth popular culture, pedagogy, and curriculum in urban classrooms, *The Review of Education, Pedagogy, and Cultural Studies, 26,* 312–337. doi: 10.1080/10714410490905366

Facebook. (2011). *Statistics.* Retrieved from http://www.facebook.com/press/info. php?statistics

Forehand, M. (2005). Bloom's taxonomy: Original and revised. In M. Orey (Ed.), *Emerging Perspectives on Learning, Teaching, and Technology.* Department of Educational Psychology and Instructional Technology, University of Georgia. Retrieved from http://projects.coe.uga.edu/epltt/

Freire, P., & Macedo, D. (1987). *Literacy: Reading the word & the world.* Westport, CT: Bergin & Garvey.

Furco, A., & Root, S. (2010). Research demonstrates the value of service learning, *Phi Delta Kappan,* 91, 16–20. Retrieved from http://www.pdkintl.org/kappan/index.htm

Gladwell, M. (2010, October 4). Small change: Why the revolution will not be tweeted. *New Yorker Magazine.* Retrieved from http://www.newyorker.com/reporting/2010/10/04/ 101004fa_fact_gladwell#ixzz17qjJws6f

Greene, M. (1995). *Releasing the imagination: Essays on education, the arts, and social change.* San Francisco: John Wiley & Sons.

Kessler, S. (2010). *Seven fantastic free social media tools for teachers.* Mashable. Retrieved from http://mashable.com/2010/10/16/free-social-media-tools-for-teachers/.

Kielsmeier, J. (2010). Build a bridge between service and learning, *Phi Delta Kappan,* 91, 8–15. Retrieved from http://www.pdkintl.org

Levy, J. (2010). *Microblogging.* Retrieved from http://www.usa.gov/webcontent/technology/microblogging.shtml

Lewis, B., & Richardson, S. (2008). *Service-learning and social media.* Retrieved from http://spotlight.macfound.org/blog/entry/lewis-richardson-service-learning-social-media/

Lewis, J. (2008). Reflections on a dream deferred. *Teaching Tolerance, 33.* Retrieved from http://www.tolerance.org/magazine/number-33-spring-2008/reflections-dream-deferred

Melchior, A. (2009). Earth Force: Youth for a change! *Summary of 2008–2009 evaluation results.* Waltham, MA: Center for Youth and Communities, Brandeis University.

National Service Learning Clearinghouse. (2010). *What is service-learning?* Retrieved from http://www.servicelearning.org/what_is_service-learning/service-learning_is

National Youth Leadership Council. (2007). *Growing to greatness 2007: The state of service-learning project.* St. Paul, MN: National Youth Leadership Council. Retrieved from http://servicelearning.org/filemanager/download/7176_Growing_to_Greatness_2007.pdf

New Commission on the Skills of the American Workforce. (2006). *Tough choices or tough times: The report of the new commission on the skills of the American workforce.* Washington, DC: National Center on Education and the Economy.

Postman, N. (2004). The information age: A blessing or a curse? The *Harvard International Journal of Press/Politics, 9*(3). Retrieved from http://hij.sagepub.com/content/9/2/3.citation. doi: 10.1177/1081180X04263457.

Pryor, J.H., Hurtado, S., DeAngelo, L., Palucki-Blake, L., & Tran, S. (2009). *The American freshman: National norms fall 2009.* Los Angeles, CA: Higher Education Research Institute, UCLA. Retrieved from http://www.heri.ucla.edu/PDFs/pubs/briefs/brief-pr012110-09FreshmanNorms.pdf

Putnam, R.D. (1995). Tuning in, tuning out: The strange disappearance of social capital in America. *Political Science and Politics, 28*(4), 664–683. Retrieved from http://apsanet3b.inetu.net/imgtest/PSDec95Putnam.pdf.

RMC Research Corporation. (2007). *Reflection in K–12 service-learning.* Scotts Valley, CA: National Service-Learning Clearinghouse. Retrieved from http://www.servicelearning.org/instant_info/fact_sheets/k-12_facts/reflection

Swartz, O., Campbell, K., & Pestana, C. (2009). Neo-pragmatism, communication, and the culture of creative democracy. New York, NY: Peter Lang.

Thompson, C. (2009, September 17). Clive Thompson on the new literacy. *Wired Magazine.* Retrieved from http://www.wired.com/print/techbiz/people/magazine/17-09/st_thompson

Vygotsky, L.S. (1978). *Mind in society: The development of higher psychological processes.* Cambridge, MA: Harvard University Press.

APPENDIX

Social Media Tips for Earth Force Six Step Process

This section is a reference tool that educators can use as they progress through the Earth Force six-step process. Each tip provides an opportunity for the educator to enrich the service-learning experience for their students and community partners.

The Launch

1. Have students use flipcams to record how they define their community. Upload those videos to YouTube, TeacherTube, Vimeo or other video sharing sites and compare with one another to help construct a collective definition of community.

2. Host a blog or chat where students read examples of high-quality service-learning projects and discuss qualities of community problem solvers that they see within those examples.

Step 1: Community Inventory

1. Use Twitter or other microblogging communication to ask for input from people within the community about their perceptions of important issues and strengths.

2. Post media links to a class blog where students can start a discussion thread on what strengths and issues they see in the stories.

Step 2: Issue Selection

1. Host a vote on Survey Monkey (www.surveymonkey.com) to narrow down identification of issues. Post the survey link on the class blog or web page to ask input from others.

Step 3: Policy and Practice Research

1. Use social media outlet search functions to see who is talking about the same issues. Search for key terms related to the issue and explore the search results for information to help inform the research.

Step 4: Strategy Selection

1. Return to the stakeholders and resources from various social media outlets and get ideas about how other communities have addressed similar issues. No need to reinvent the wheel! The work of others can provide many ideas for strategies for change.

Step 5: Taking Action

1. Post action plans and project stories on one of several service-learning websites.
2. Have students record one another taking action and then construct it into a video that portrays their progress.
3. Use social media outlets to promote actions taken to address an issue. Put out a call to action for others to follow suit.

Step 6: Looking Back and Ahead

1. Invite stakeholders to view student documentation of their process and progress to provide community feedback through the class blog, web site, or social media outlets that have been used throughout the process.
2. Use photos and video clips collected along the way to create a process documentation video to upload and share. Send a copy to all stakeholders that have been involved as well.
3. Create podcasts of tips on addressing community issues to share. What were intentional and unintended learning experiences that students can share with others who want to take action in their own communities?

CHAPTER 8

DESIGN PRINCIPLES FOR PROBLEM-DRIVEN INSTRUCTION WITH ONLINE SOCIAL MEDIA IN KOREAN CONTEXTS

Jihyun Si and Dongsik Kim

Collaborative learning in online social media fosters interaction between participants. This networked learning has become an integrated part of everyday learning in higher educational settings. Recently, a number of newly emergent online social media have widely been used, and incorporating more and more newly developed devices into educational settings seems unavoidable. However, collaborative learning theory should guide practitioners and researchers to make the best decisions in order to promote the desired collaborative learning regardless of types of tools such as PCs, smartphones, wikis, or apps. Unlike well-structured traditional school tasks, authentic, complex, ill-structured problems encourage sharing and negotiating ideas due to their ill-structured features. Collaborative learning environments with online social media may offer suitable places for such collaborative efforts. However, interaction that occurs in online social media should not be taken for granted.

Designing Problem-Driven Instruction with Online Social Media, pages 147–168
Copyright © 2012 by Information Age Publishing
147

All the components of collaborative learning should be taken into careful consideration. Therefore, we propose design principles for problem-driven instructions with online social media based on collaborative learning theory, particularly in Korean contexts.

INTRODUCTION

The main focus of this chapter is to suggest design principles that optimize problem-driven instruction with online social media, especially in Korean contexts. Online social media are new ways to improve participants' interactive discourse by using web-based and mobile technologies. Collaborative learning with online social media is "an interdisciplinary research field focused on how collaborative learning, supported by technology, can enhance peer interaction and work in groups, and how collaboration and technology facilitate sharing and distributing knowledge and expertise among community members" (Lipponen, Hakkarainen, & Paavola, 2004, p. 32). Wherever this networked learning is implemented, for example, either in PC or smartphones, or on wikis or apps on smartphones, collaborative learning theory should guide practitioners and researchers to make the best decisions that promote desired collaborative learning.

The implementation of this networked learning has become an integrated part of everyday learning in higher educational settings (De Graaff, De Laat, & Scheltinga, 2004). One of the essential goals for higher education is helping college students develop into professionals who are able to deal with complex, ill-structured problems based on the real world. Text-based asynchronous collaborative learning environments with online social media facilitate negotiation and reflection, so they offer suitable places for collaborative ill-structured problem solving.

In Korea, some research on collaborative learning with online social media has been conducted in teacher education contexts in college to scrutinize the effects of a grounding supporting tool in wiki-based collaborative learning environments (Kim, 2009; Sun, 2010); scripts for collaborative argumentation in online collaborative learning environments (Bhang, 2009); the display of both qualitative and quantitative data of learners' participation (Ko, 2010); and the types of collaboration scripts on collaboration load, collaboration process, and outcomes (Jung, 2010). These studies examined parts of collaborative knowledge construction processes and provided insights for design principles for problem-driven instruction with online social media. However, to develop and refine a feasible instruction that could enhance college students' argumentative knowledge construction, comprehensive design principles for collaborative learning with online social media are necessary. Thus, this chapter will first conceptualize collaborative learning theory and nature of problem-driven learning. Then, based on what we have reviewed and the research recently conducted in Korea, we will suggest the design principles for problem-driven instruction with online social media as a means of leveraging the potential of current and emerging online collaborative tools in teacher education program contexts in higher education settings in Korea.

COLLABORATIVE LEARNING
COMPONENTS IN ONLINE SOCIAL MEDIA

Three Frameworks for Understating Collaborative Learning

In early studies, learning in groups was treated as a fundamentally individual process and working in groups as a variable of having impact on individual learning (Dillenbourg, Baker, Blaye, & O'Malley, 1996). However, Roschelle and Teasley (1995) suggested that "collaboration is a coordinated, synchronous activity that is the result of a continued attempt to construct and maintain a shared conception of a problem" (p. 70). In other words, learning happens as the collaborative construction of knowledge through negotiation (Stahl, Koschmann, & Suthers, 2006). Thus, the characteristics of collaboration such as collaborative negotiation and social sharing show that both individual and group processes need to be considered as units of learning in collaborative learning (Stahl et al., 2006).

Sfard (1998) suggested two metaphors for learning to establish frameworks for understanding the practices and orientations of collaborative learning: the acquisition metaphor and the participation metaphor. Lipponen et al. (2004) added a third metaphor, the knowledge creation metaphor. According to the acqusition framwork, learning is considered as construction, acquisition, and outcomes and is a process that implants knowledge into our mind (Sfard, 1998). Knowledge is seen as a property of individual minds, so the unit of anlysis is individual or dyad (Lipponen et al., 2004; Sfard, 1998). In contrast, "the participation metaphor based on the situated cognition approach sees learning as participation in various cultural practices and shared learning activities" (Paavola, Lipponen, & Hakkarainen, 2004, p. 557). In this approach, knowing (activities) is more focused than knowledge (outcomes), and knowledge and knowing cannot be detached from situations where they take place or are utilized (Cobb, & Bowers, 1999; Lipponen et al., 2004). Interaction, discourse, and participation among community members in a certain context are the center of the participation framework (Lave & Wenger, 1991). Paavola et al. (2004) argued that the two frameworks are not enough to capture all the aspects of collaborative learning. In addition, Bereiter (2002) claimed that the acquisition framework cannot say anything about knowledge that does not exist in the individual mind and the participation framework, nor dictate how to go beyond best practices, nor define how new knowledge is created, and he offered the idea of knowledge building as a solution. Based on Bereiter (2002) and Engeström (1987), Paavola et al. (2004) proposed the knowledge creation metaphor. This metaphor concerns how new knowledge or practices are created by collaborative activities, which was not focused on with the other two metaphors. The knowledge creation metaphor concentrates on mediated processes of knowledge creation, and learning is understood as a collaborative effort toward generating artifacts including ideas, practices, and conceptual artifacts (Paavola et al, 2004). In this framework, ideas are expressed, and mediated through a rich variety of representational tools such as language, computers, and models. Moreover, they are expanded and progressed by collaborative activities organized around shared objects rather than taking place through immediate interaction between participants (Lipponen, et al., 2004). Individual activities are also stressed in this framework but as a part of social stream of activities, not individually separately (Lipponen et al., 2004). Technology is considered as a mediating tool or a transformative artifact that assists learning (Lipponen, et al., 2004).

Collaboration Scripts

To create new knowledge or practices, learners need to be involved in collaborative learning activities. The problem lies in the fact that learners do not collaborate well when they are left to their own devices (King, 2007). Without some form of explicit guidance to induce productive interaction, learners tend to interact with each other at the very basic level. They rarely engage in such as asking questions, clarifying and justifying their opinions, expressing their reasoning, and elaborating and reflecting on their knowledge (Kobbe et al., 2007). In these situations, collaboration scripts can be one method of explicit guidance. Collaboration scripts intend to "foster collaborative learning by shaping the way in which learners interact with one another. In specifying a sequence of learning activities, together with appropriate roles for the learners, collaboration scripts are designed to trigger engagement in social and cognitive activities that would otherwise occur rarely or not at all" (Kobbe et al, 2007. p. 212).

Collaboration scripts have proven to be powerful strategies for supporting collaborative learning in problem-solving contexts (King, 2007; Rummel, & Spada, 2007). However, regarding what specific aspects of collaboration should be guided, different researchers have different notions. In general, the two main focal points of research and design are distinguished as the macro and micro level (Dillenbourg, & Jermann, 2007; Fischer, Kollar, Haake, & Mandl, 2007; Haake, & Pfister, 2007). A micro-script reflects a psychological perspective and scaffolds the interaction process—mostly argumentation process embedded in environments—which learners are expected to progressively internalize (Dillenbourg, & Hong, 2006). For example, a collaboration script leads learners to produce a counter-argument to the argument of their peers (Weinberger, Stegmann, Fischer, & Mandl, 2007). On the other hand, the macro-script reflects an educational perspective and affects the organizational issues of collaborative learning such as forming groups in a specific way, or scripting the collaboration process using specific phases, roles, and activities (Dillenbourg, & Hong, 2006).

In collaboration settings in online social media, scripts can be incorporated into interface design to provide optimal environments for productive collaboration (Rummel & Spada, 2007). For example, an interface requires participants to choose contribution types from predefined menus and then allows them to write their specific contribution. Also, participants are asked to indicate which contribution their contribution is relating to (Haake, & Pfister, 2007). This kind of scripting could exert a high degree of coercion on the collaborators (Dilenbourg, 2002). Dilenbourg (2002) expressed concerns about a danger to overscript. That is, how coercive should the script be? Scripts vary by the degree of freedom learners have in following the script. According to Dilenbourg (2002), a "certain degree of coercion is required for efficiency reasons, but too much might be in contradiction with the very idea of collaborative learning and might decrease student motivation" (p. 80). Finding an optimal extent of coercion in which learners are actively involved in collaborative activities while at the same time their initiative is not interrupted may be essential to design effective collaborative learning environments.

Collaboration Mechanism

Organizations increasingly use multidisciplinary teams for solving complex problems collaboratively as different perspectives allow rich problem analyses and solutions (Kirschner, Beers, Boshuizen, & Gijselaers, 2008). However, multidisciplinary is not always beneficial. Bromme (2000) argued that good team solutions call for a good degree of common ground among team members. Common ground indicates some kind of commonality among members of multidisciplinary teams. Once achieved, it serves as a shared cognitive frame of reference among collaborators (Bromme, 2000).

Beers, Boshuizen, Kirschner, and Gijselaers (2005) hypothesized that to construct knowledge based on achievement of common ground, "the route from unshared knowledge in one participant's head to newly constructed knowledge in a team goes through three intermediate forms (i.e., external knowledge, shared knowledge, and common ground) via four processes, externalization, internalization, negotiation and integration" (p. 625). First, the unshared knowledge in participants' heads is externalized through contributions to discussion. Then, other participants try to internalize the knowledge based on consideration of aspects of the contributors such as their background, current situations and their own beliefs and assumption (Bromme, 2000). From a shared contribution, negotiation of common ground occurs. Beers et al. (2005) also suggested a set of communication rules to negotiate meaning and positions. According to this communication model, "new conversation topics are introduced via contribution message and then, verified and clarified using verification and clarification messages. Furthermore, participants can use agree- and disagree- messages to make their position known to their teammates, and can post rejections to messages that are unintelligible" (Kirschner et al., 2008, p. 407).

From the established common ground, new knowledge is constructed and elaborated through integration. The common constructed knowledge becomes part of the common ground and denotes the solutions in problem-solving contexts (Beers et al, 2005).

Collaborative Activities

For successful collaborative learning, group members need to engage in different types of activities. Group members have to perform task-specific activities aimed at solving the problem at hand. These task-related activities stimulate successful problem solving and individual learning. Second, group members need "social interaction necessary for socio-emotional processes such as affiliation, getting to know each other, developing social relationship with peers and creating a social space of trust, belonging and where a sense of community exist" (Kreijns & Kirschner, 2004, p. 225). Such solid social space and sense of belonging nurture supporting atmosphere which is a prerequisite for critical dialogues (Kreijns & Kirschner, 2004). As a result, group members' efforts to complete the group task will increase (Rourke, Anderson, Garrison, & Archer, 1999).

Third, group members need to engage in coordination or regulation of task-related activities (Erkens, 2004; Erkens, Jaspers, Prangsma, & Kanselaar, 2005). Coordination of task-related activities means "making them happen in the right order and at the right time to complete the task without conflicting with others in the group" (Gutwin & Greenberg, 2004, p. 9). That is, metacognitive activities that control task performance, such as making plans and monitoring task progress, are considered significant to successful collaborative learning. Finally, collaboration also requires coordination or regulation of social activities (Erkens, 2004). During collaboration, group members are interdependent, so they need to converse about collaboration strategies and the collaboration process, and evaluate and reflect on the manner of their collaboration (Janssen, Erkens, Kanselaar, & Jaspers, 2006).

Visualization of Participation

The high level of participation and equality of participation in online collaborative learning may be key components of successful collaborative learning. Visualization of participation in online collaborative learning may be an effective strategy to stimulate the high level and equality of participation (Janssen et al., 2006). Visualizing the level of participation of group members makes the contribution of each group member explicit to the others. As their participation becomes transparent to other group members, participants are motivated to actively participate, which serves to counter the free rider effect (Johnson, & Johnson, 1999). It is also assumed that they will participate more to avoid negative evaluation from other team members by insufficient participation (Janssen et al., 2006).

Furthermore, visualization of participation can also be regarded as a form of external feedback. This feedback about "how well they are collaborating, and whether they have selected an appropriate collaboration strategy...how well their group is functioning and how group processes may be improved" (Janssen et al, 2006, p. 5) can be used by learners to monitor their problem-solving progress. Students' awareness can also be raised of the activities participants are involved in (Janssen et al, 2006). Students need to know which activities their group members participate in during collaboration to choose which activities to be involved in. The research of Gutwin and Greenberg (2004) and Kirschner, Strijbos, Kreijns and Beers (2004) showed that participants' awareness of group process has positive influence in facilitating collaborative learning in online social media.

Managing Collaborative Load

Dillenbourg and Betrancourt (2006) argued that any computer-mediated learning environment imposes an additional cognitive load on learners, especially at the outset of its use. They contended that "in CSCL, this computer interaction additional load is increased with the social interaction load or collaborative load (i.e. the need to manage interactions with the other group members)" (p. 144). According to the Cognitive Load Theory (Sweller, 1998), "learning environments for complex cognitive tasks can only be effective and efficient when they are designed in such a way that they facilitate changes in learners' long-term memory associated with schema construction and schema automation" (Janssen, Kirschner, Erkens, Kirschner, & Paas, 2010, p. 144). The processing capacity of a learner's working memory is limited, so if a learning task is too difficult, schema construction will not occur (Janssen et al, 2010). Thus, effective and efficient collaborative learning takes place only if cognitive resources are sufficient to cover the processing requirements.

For a group to carry out a learning task, not all participants need to possess all the necessary knowledge or information. Through communication and coordination between group members, associated labor and cognitive load can be divided among group members (Janssen et al., 2010). This distribution will impose less cognitive load on collaborating individuals. Conversely, the inter-individual communication and coordination processes such as verbalization of thoughts, the construction of shared understanding, and the maintenance of a representation of the other members' thoughts may impose additional cognitive load on group members (Dillenbourg & Betrancourt, 2006; Janssen et al., 2010). For effective collaborative learning, the distribution advantage needs to be large enough to compensate for the extraneous cognitive load imposed due to ineffective transaction among members (Janssen et al., 2010).

Text-based Communication

Online collaborative learning environments are mainly based on asynchronous text-based commination. Participants type to communicate and read messages onscreen at their own convenient time (Weinberger, 2008). The messages are recorded on a central database and are typically represented in discussion threads. These threads start with one message about a specific subject matter indicated by the title, and the author and other members may further build on it. These build-on messages are indented and are graphically connected to an initial message. New subjects are set off with a new discussion thread. These structured messages organized around a topic are archived and help learners locate knowledge resources to form groups of interest and to produce answers to complex problems (Scardamalia & Bereiter, 1996).

The separate spaces for specific purposes can be built in online collaborative learning environments such as online cafes for informal conversation spaces, virtual information centers to inform new community members how to use the environment, virtual libraries for the collected archives of the community, and so on (Weinberger, 2008). These virtual spaces aim to support the accumulation of a certain type of knowledge. Effective knowledge management within the context of ongoing educational processes can lead to both successful learning and the creation of more stable relationships among members based on knowledge sharing. As a result, the value of the individual contribution to growing shared knowledge structures is amplified (Weinberger, 2008).

NATURE OF PROBLEM-SOLVING PERFORMANCE

Good Problems

Kirschner et al. (2008) argued that tasks used in collaborative learning are not often suited to collaboration; they are often too closed to stimulate further discussion, too easy to be dealt with by a team, or too controlled for learners to take the initiative (Kirschner et al., 2008). Then, what are good problems for collaborative learning? Duch (2001) suggested characteristics of a good problem for problem-driven learning. An effective problem should interest students, motivate them, and promote argumentation. It should also be open-ended, controversial, and complex enough that collaborators negotiate meaning through interactions with other team members and effectively work toward a solution as a group. Also, the problem should incorporate objectives of course content and find connection between previous knowledge and new concepts and between new knowledge and concepts in other courses. It must also be realistic and resonate with the students' experience (Jonassen, 1997).

Problems also need to be ill-structured (Jonassen, 1997). Most problems in everyday and professional practices are ill-structured, not well-defined. Ill-structured problems are not clearly defined, nor is the prerequisite information enclosed in the problem statement. Their solutions are unpredictable, unlimited to one subject area, and could be many (Jonassen, 1997). As ill-structured problems are based on real-life contexts, they are more interesting and meaningful to learners.

Problem Representation

Jonassen (2003) claimed, "Problem solvers need to construct some sort of internal representation (mental model) of a problem in order to solve a problem" (p. 365). To form a suitable internal representation that strengthens conceptual understanding, learners should be encouraged to view a problem from different perspectives (Jonassen, 2003). If they depend solely on any single form of representation constructed based on one perspective, students' understanding of the problem and its relationship to the domain knowledge may be constrained. As experts construct richer, more integrated mental representations of problems than do novices, they are the better problem solvers (Jonassen, 2003). The given instruction must help learners construct multiple problem representations based on the understanding of the internal connections between problems and domain knowledge. Then, the effects of using technology tools to externally represent problems on collaborative problem solving contexts are expected to be great. In addition, Jonassen (2003) argued that external representation of problems decreases collaborative load. Sweller and Chandler (1994) argued that while learners are solving complex problems, their limited working memory is an obstacle to coping with multiple elements of information given simultaneously. Providing an external representation of the problem components may support their working memory by decreasing elements of a problem simultaneously dealt with.

Problem-driven Collaborative Learning with Online Social Media

In problem-driven collaborative learning, learners are expected to solve given or emerging problems together. Students may represent components and dimensions of the problem, generate hypotheses about possible solutions, apply those possible solutions, and evaluate their hypotheses. At the completion of each problem solving, students reflect on the abstract knowledge gained (Hmelo-Silver, 2004). In this process, argumentation is an essential skill. Especially in solving ill-structured problems, the production of coherent argumentation to justify solutions and actions is an essential skill (Cho & Jonassen, 2002). Because ill-structured problems do not have merging answers or constant solution criteria, learners must construct arguments to defend their own assumptions, solution paths, and proposed solutions (Jonassen, 1997). However, as discussed previously, learners neither voluntarily work well on collaborative learning tasks nor interact productively (Weinberger et al., 2007). Kuhn, Shaw and Felton's (1997) research showed that adult discussants rarely warrant or qualify their claims and thus rarely construct complete arguments. Therefore, the pedagogical structures are necessary for supporting collaborative argumentation.

Collaborative learning with online social media is regarded as a suitable context for facilitating argumentative knowledge construction (Weinberger et al, 2007). In text-based asynchronous communication, learners may compensate for lack of learning prerequisites by investing more time in the reception and production of individual contributions. Learners may also take advantage of instructional supports provided as part of the communication interface such as scripts (Weinberger, 2008). Scripts can constrain conversations and discourses among collaborators with the aim to guide the exchange of knowledge and information (Beers et al, 2005). Specific scripts are coined to facilitate specific aspects of problem solving such as complex reasoning, task-oriented activities, and collaborative knowledge construction, and learners are coerced to follow such rules (Dillenbourg, 2002).

Another key issue related to online collaborative learning is that the roles of the student and teacher are transformed. The teachers are facilitators in online collaborative problem-solving contexts (Hmelo-Silver, 2004). They are no longer considered as the main source of knowledge. Teachers guide the learning process by, for example, asking open-ended questions, encouraging students to make their thinking visible, and keeping all the students participating in the group process (Hmelo-Silver, 2004). Students also become more responsible for their own learning through reflective, self-directed learning processes (Bereiter, 2002).

DESIGN PRINCIPLES FOR PROBLEM-DRIVEN INSTRUCTION WITH ONLINE SOCIAL MEDIA

The use of online social media has expanded greatly in the past decade, but instead of adopting or inventing new technologies specifically tuned to collaborative learning, pre-existing Internet technology has too often been applied to deliver traditional pedagogical approaches to collaborative learning environments (Suthers, Vatrapu, Medina, Joseph, & Dwyer, 2008). Online social media should support collaborative knowledge construction, leveraging the computational medium's strengths such as its representational capabilities, its interactivity, and its structured or networked support for collaborative learning (Suthers et al., 2008). In this section, based on what we have previously reviewed and the research recently conducted in teacher education contexts in Korean higher education settings, we will suggest design principles for problem-driven instruction with online social media, and then we will offer further suggestions especially tailored for Korean education settings.

Principle 1: Provide Collaboration Scripts for Argumentative Knowledge Construction

As mentioned earlier, learners need support for effective collaboration. Through collaboration scripts, learners are guided to enter activities that nurture productive interaction and collaborative knowledge construction. Bhang (2009) examined the effects of scripts with 102 students enrolled in preservice teacher training courses in a college. She developed a computer-supported collaborative argumentation environment and embedded the scripts for collaborative argumentation into the environment. She argued that scripts should reflect on collaborative knowledge construction mechanisms to avoid superficial argumentation among learners. Moreover, scripts should be provided as an integrated form able to support the sequence of argumentative conversations, the structuring of a single argumentation, and the skills for argumentative thinking all together. The results of the study showed that the integrated scripts were effective for forming counter-arguments and synthesizing their initial positions into integration. It also showed that collaborative argumentative scripts promoted the sharing of knowledge among group members and the individual acquisition of domain knowledge.

Weinberger et al. (2007) also examined the effects of scripts for argumentative knowledge construction. However, they suggested that computer-supported scripts that target a specific process can facilitate the specific process and outcomes of argumentative knowledge construction during collaboration instead of "one-script-fits-all" (Weinberger et al., 2007, p. 206). Their results advocated their claim. The epistemic script components helped learners to construct arguments that contribute to solving problem cases; the argumentative script components supported argumentative knowledge construction; and the social script components facilitated the dimension of social modes of co-construction of argumentative knowledge construction.

To find out which way is more effective, either one dimension at a time or one-script-fits-all, further investigation is necessary. However, learners hardly construct well-grounded arguments in collaborative argumentative knowledge construction without any help (Stegmann, Weinberger, & Fischer, 2007), so solely providing opportunities for learners to engage in argumentative debate is insufficient. Offering either a single script coined for a specific goal dimension or one integrated script designed to support sequence, structure, and skills for collaborative argumentation may be essential for learners to benefit from participating in collaborative learning.

Principle 2: Externally Represent Problem Space for Solid Common Ground Building

Solving complex problems might benefit from working with multidisciplinary teams considering multiple perspectives of complex ill-structured problems. Team interaction is directly related to its performance, and constructing a shared problem space seemed to be essential for engaging multiple perspectives (Barron, 2003). To build solid common ground, a shared cognitive frame of reference (Barron, 2003), individual knowledge needs to be externally represented for negotiation among members. In Kim's (2009) study on designing an argumentation supporting tool in wiki-based CSCL, she provided an argumentation graph as an external representation tool to learners enrolled in preservice teacher education programs and discovered that the provision of external representations was effective in articulating argumentation processes and negotiating meanings. Also, the argumentation graph made it easier for learners to take a close look at the flow of arguments and argument construction. Similarly, Sun (2010) conducted research about the effects of the grounding supporting tool in interaction among leaners and collaborative knowledge construction in wiki-based CSCL. The result indicated that the group provided with the grounding supporting tool, the question-and-answer activity, wrote significantly more on-task messages, whereas the control group wrote more massages for coordination. Thus, he concluded that the grounding supporting tool facilitated the meaningful interaction between participants and as a result, facilitated the activities for collaborative knowledge building.

External representation initiates negotiation of meaning (Suthers, 2001). When individuals want to add to or modify a shared representation, they may feel they need to attain agreement from other group members, which leads to negotiations to justify their modifications. The components of a collaboratively constructed representation can evoke rich meanings an individual participant does not intend. They also guide the search for new knowledge by making missing knowledge salient. Furthermore, the external representation serves as an easy way to refer to ideas previously developed (Suthers, 2001).

Principle 3: Visualize Both Quantitative and Qualitative Data of Participation of Participants

Visualization of participation can contribute to successful collaborative learning in online social media (Janssen et al., 2006; Janssen, Erkens, & Kanselaar, 2007). Through displaying the degree of participation visually, individual accountability is seemingly stressed, therefore preventing the free rider effect. The study of Janssen et al. (2006) showed that visualizing how much each group member contributes to the group's online discussion encouraged the participants to participate more and more equally.

To improve awareness of group processes, the information of how they are interacting or what activities they are involved in is equally as important as how often they contribute. In other words, both qualitative and quantitative data about participants' participation are important to promote active participation during collaboration. Ko (2010) conducted research on the effect of both qualitative and quantitative data with forty students enrolled in preservice teacher training programs in college. She developed an awareness tool and displayed it on the first page of the online learning environment; whenever learners logged onto the website, they could see the display. The participants exchanged, shared, and discussed what they researched for the class presentation through a chat tool and online discussion board. The degree of participation and the discussion messages are collected and analyzed every day and provided to learners as quantitative data such as frequency of contribution to the online discussion and qualitative data about activities that learners engaged in such as providing relevant information, knowledge recreation, and group progressing. The result showed that the group provided with both quantitative and qualitative data showed a higher rate of participation than groups provided either quantitative data or qualitative data. Therefore, visualizing may augment students' participation, but visualizing only quantitative aspects of collaboration may not be sufficient. Through visualizing both qualitative and quantitative aspects of participation, leaners can see the whole picture of their participation, which may encourage more active and equal participation.

Principle 4: Provide Tools to Support Social Interaction

Social affordance in online social media means the environmental characteristics accountable for the degree and type of social interaction (Kreijns

& Kirschner, 2004). For example, once a group member is online, aware-ness tools graphically display who is online, which can stimulate informal conversation (Kreijns & Kirschner, 2004). Such social affordance devices can increase the number of impromptu exchanges and bridge the time gap due to asynchronous communication (Kreijns & Kirschner, 2004). This device is integrated in non-task contexts as well as in task contexts. The provision of the devices in non-task contexts allows casual and informal conversations such as conversations before a coffee machine at school and provides chances to exchange not only task-related information but also socio-emotional information, which may lead to developing trust, social cohesiveness, and a sense of belonging to the group. This rapport in turn facilitates critical thinking processes carried out by the group members.

Social presence is another important concept related to social interaction in collaborative learning with online social media. Garrison, Anderson, and Archer (2000) define social presence as the "ability of participants in the community of inquiry to project their personal characteristics into the com-munity, thereby presenting themselves to the other participants as [a] real person" (p. 4). If the media provide more channels for learners to project themselves, their social presence increases, and this increased social presence can positively affect online social interaction. Garrsion et al. (2000) claimed that social presence not only indirectly facilitates the critical thinking pro-cesses carried on by participants but may also make them remain in the co-hort of learners during collaboration. In this way, social presence directly contributes to the success of collaborative learning with online social media. Therefore, providing tools to improve social presence is another critical com-ponent for effective and productive collaborative learning.

Principle 5: Manage Collaborative Load by Guiding Collaboration Processes

Collaboration imposes an additional task on the learners—that is, man-aging interpersonal relations and group functioning. Collaboration scripts may help reduce collaborative efforts by imposing rules of how to inter-act or providing guidance on how to collaborate or how to solve problems (Suthers, 2007). Jung's (2010) study showed how to control cognitive load with collaboration scripts. She sampled 51 college students enrolled in preservice teacher training programs and studied the impact on them of three different collaboration scripts embedded in online learning environ-ments on collaboration load, process, and outcomes. She hypothesized that providing a collaboration model (an exemplary collaboration activ-ity) with explanation activities to peers would optimize their collaboration loads as it can curb the occurrence of inefficient interaction, facilitate com-mon ground creation, and encourage reflection and elaboration of their thought through explanation. The result of Jung's study (2010) empirically showed that the group provided with the collaboration model with an explanation activity to peers gained significantly lower scores in interaction-related extraneous load and earned significantly higher scores in domain knowledge acquisition than the groups provided with only collaboration model, or a collaboration model with a self-explanation activity. That is, collaboration scripts, including explanation activities to peers, played a significant role in decreasing unnecessary interaction and effectively building common ground among the learners, therefore, leading to optimizing their collaboration load.

Dillenbourg and Betrancourt (2006) argued that "the goal of the CSCL designer is to tune this collaboration load within an acceptable range, i.e., above a floor threshold below which too few cognitive processes are triggered but below a ceiling threshold (overload) above which collaboration becomes painful or unmanageable" (p. 153). The interaction that enables students to construct knowledge is not free of charge, but any collaboration load that goes beyond the optimal collaborative effort makes collaboration excessively difficult (Dillenbourg & Betrancourt, 2006).

Principle 6: Provide Tools to Organize Discussion Threads

The shared agreement or knowledge constructed through discourse is not always made explicit by typical web-based communication tools for collaborative learning. Thus, it is difficult to find relevant contributions, place one's own contribution into the relevant context, or quickly assess the outcome of the discourse (Suthers, 2001). Providing tools for sorting notes by writer, date, and knowledge type in discussion thread might help learners follow the knowledge-building discourses and improve coherence as the conceptual reference of each contribution (Suthers, 2001). In addition, a tool to collect items from broad discussion and organize them flexibly according to various perspectives is necessary for further manipulation of data and sharing.

Principle 7: Keep Archives and Embed a Search Engine in Learning Environments

Learners need diverse supporting data to justify their claim in argumentation. If learners can have easy access to various data including text, image, and videos from diverse sources, they may easily recognize the existence of alternative opinions and perspectives, which is critical to deepening their conceptual understanding. That is, by examining previously worked examples in archives or searching for further information with an embedded search engine, they can be exposed to cognitive diversity and variation in the fields of expertise, which can lead to promoting knowledge advancement and cognitive growth.

Principle 8: Provide Authentic, Complex, Ill-structured Problems

Solving problems is one of the most important skills for everyday life. While working collaboratively with other team members, group members need to deal with cognitive conflict, elaborate on each other's contributions, and construct shared representations and meaning to solve the problem (Kirschner et al., 2004). However, not all types of problems are worth all the collaboration efforts leaners need to exert on working collaboratively. Traditional school tasks are not authentic in that they are usually very well-structured, short in length, well-defined, individual-oriented, and designed to best fit the school content (Kirschner et al., 2004). Authentic, complex, ill-structured problems that can accommodate multiple perspectives are suited to collaborative learning.

Principle 9: Provide Channels for Learners to Interact Each Other Directly

Learners are expected to be self-directed, effective, intrinsically motivated collaborators in problem-driven learning situations in online social media (Hmelo-Silver, 2004). Thus, teachers do not have to be a "sage on the stage" in such situations. They, as facilitators, need to guide the argumentative knowledge construction by encouraging leaners to justify and reflect on their thinking or get involved in online interaction (Hmelo-Silver, 2004). By offering multiple paths for students to interact with each other directly and providing artifacts for them to interact with, the teacher should avoid the situations where all communication must go through the teacher and all progress depends on teachers dispensing knowledge (Stahl, 2004).

Further Suggestions for Korean Contexts

In addition to the universal principles for designing problem-driven instruction with online social media, we would like to offer three more suggestions especially tailored to Korean educational contexts. First, in most of the studies in Korean contexts cited before, students were asked to discuss a topic provided, not generate an artifact or a solution. From the knowledge creation metaphor as discussed in the previous section, learning is regarded as a collaborative effort toward generating artifacts or solutions for complex problems. Topics asking just to discuss a problem are not enough to integrate their discussions into knowledge construction and may make debating superficial. Furthermore, many portions of activities in the research were asked to be completed individually, which in turn resulted in fewer opportunities for getting involved in group discussions. Thus, organizing discussion threads in diverse ways, keeping archives, and embedding a search engine for further profound discussions were not regarded as important components in the studies. The goal for collaborative problem-based learning is for students to publicly articulate their current state of understanding, generate hypotheses for problem solving, defend them to others in their group, and integrate ideas as a group. To do so, the authentic, complex problem solving should be a driving force for learning, and collaborative learning environments with online social media should be carefully designed to encourage collaborative activities for problem solving.

Another issue particularly related to students in Korea is the degree of coerciveness of scripts. That is, how coercive should scripts be? Specific communication patterns depending on different cultures exist, according to Hall and Hall (1990). Si (2005) conducted research on the first-time online leaner's role adjustment patterns in online learning contexts based on Hall and Hall's (1990) high- and low-context culture model. According to the results, learners from the high-context cultures including Korea needed more teacher intervention to be satisfied with online learning experiences, as students from high-context cultures (or larger power distance cultures; see Hall & Hall, 1990 for comprehensive discussions) are highly dependent on teachers for their learning. Si argued that increasing teacher presence, such as more instructional supports at the beginning of a course, had a great positive influence for their successful learning experience. Then, regarding designing collaboration scripts, relatively more structured scripts or a lesser degree of freedom might be an effective approach for Korean students to be actively involved in collaborative activities.

Pertaining to cultural differences, social interaction deserves careful consideration as well. According to Morse's study (2003), participants in high-context cultures lamented the inability to meet with other participants in order to form social relationships, and they regarded the inability to get to know the others as both learning and social challenges. Considering this cultural inclination of emphasis on relationship in high-context cultures, the inability of text-based communication to transmit nonverbal cues is expected to have negative influences in developing social presence. Thus, providing tools to support social interaction and channels to interact with each other directly seems to be expected to have greater influences in building a sense of social presence and diminishing transactional distance among students in Korea.

CONCLUSION

The design principles for problem-driven instructions with online social media and three suggestions for Korean contexts were discussed. Kimball (1995) says, "Fruitful learning experiences do not happen by chance" (p. 54). They need to be thoughtfully designed, based on learning theory, instructional theory, and research. Thus, it is our hope that this attempt to improve our understanding of learning experiences with online social media contributes to the creation of fruitful learning experiences for all diverse participants. Newly emerging social media such as Facebook, wikis, Twitter, and so on have been growing in popularity, and their potential as useful learning tools is not small considering their feature of high inter- activity. However, very little attention has been drawn to problem-driven collaborative learning with such tools in Korea. The principles suggested in this chapter may stimulate educators, educational designers and tech- nologists, and educational researchers to reflect more profoundly on their instructional decisions in higher education settings and hopefully trigger comprehensive research to construct learning environments with online social media especially suitable for Korean contexts.

REFERENCES

Barron, B. (2003). When smart groups fail. *The Journal of the Learning Science. 12*(3), 307–359.

Beers, P. J., Boshuizen, H. P. A., Kirschner, P. A., & Gijselaers, W. H. (2005). Com- puter support for knowledge construction in collaborative learning environ- ments. *Computers in Human Behaviors, 21*, 623–643.

Bereiter, B. (2002). *Education and mind in the knowledge age.* Mawah, NJ: Lawrence Erlbaum Associates.

Bhang, S. (2009). *Effects of scaffolds for collaborative argumentation in computer-supported collaborative learning.* Unpublished doctoral dissertation, Hanyang University, Seoul, Korea.

Bromme, R. (2000). Beyond one's own perspective: The psychology of cognitive interdisciplinary. In P. Weingart & N. Stehr (Eds.), *practicing interdisciplinary* (pp. 115–133). Toronto, ON: University of Toronto Press.

Cho, K. L., & Jonassen, D. H. (2002). The effects of argumentation scaffolds on argumentation and problem-solving. *Educational Technology Research and devel- opment, 50*(3), 5–22.

Cobb, P., & Bowers, J. (1999). Cognitive and situated learning perspective and the- ory and practice. *Educational Research, 28*(2), 4–15.

De Graaff, R., De Laat, M., & Scheltinga, H. (2004). CSCL-ware in practice: goals, tasks, and constraints. In J. Strijbos, P. A. Kirschner, & R. L. Martens (Eds.), *What we know about CSCL and implementing it in higher education* (pp. 201–219). Dordrecht, The Netherlands: Kluwer Academic Publishers.

Dillenbourg, P. (2002). Over-scripting CSCL: The risks of blending collaborative learning with instructional design. In P. A. Kirschner (Ed.), *Three worlds of CSCL: Can we support CSCL?* (pp 61–91). Heerlen, The Netherlands: Open Universities Nederland.

Dillenbourg, P., Baker, M., Blaye, A., & O'Malley, C. (1996). The evolution of re- search on collaborative learning. In P. Reimann & H. Spada (Eds.), *Learn- ing in humans and machines: Towards an interdisciplinary learning science* (pp. 189–211). Oxford, UK: Elsevier.

Dillenbourg, P., & Betrancourt, M. (2006). Collaboration load. In J. Elen & R.E. Clark (Eds.), *Handling complexity in learning environments: research and theory* (pp.142–163). Oxford, UK: Elsevier Ltd.

Dillenbourg, P., & Hong, F. (2006). The mechanics of CSCL macro scripts. *Computer-Supported Collaborative Learning 3*, 5–23.

Dillenbourg, P. & Jermann, P. (2007). Designing integrative scripts. In F. Fischer, I. Kollar, H. Mandl, & J. M. Haake (Eds.), *Scripting computer-supported collaborative learning: cognitive, computational and educational perspectives* (pp. 275–301). New York, NY: Springer.

Duch, B. J. (2001). Writing problems for deeper understanding. In B. J. Duch, S. E. Groh, & D. E. Allen (Eds.), The power of problem-based learning (pp. 47–58). Sterling, VA: Stylus Publishing.

Engeström, Y. (1987). *Learning by expanding*. Helsinki: Orienta-Konsultit.

Erkens, G. (2004). Dynamics of coordination in collaboration. In J. V. der Linden & P. Renshaw (Eds.), *Dialogic learning: Shifting perspectives to learning, instruction, and teaching* (pp. 191–216). Dordrecht, The Netherlands: Kluwer Academic Publishers.

Erkens, G., Jaspers, J., Prangsma, M., & Kanselaar, G. (2005). Coordination processes in computer supported collaborative writing. *Computers in Human Behaviors, 21*(3), 463–486.

Fischer, F., Kollar, I., Haake, J. M., & Mandl, H. (2007). Perspectives on collaboration scripts. In F. Fischer, I. Kollar, H. Mandl, & J. M. Hake (Eds), *Scripting computer-supported collaborative learning: cognitive, computational and educational perspectives* (pp. 1–10). New York, NY: Springer.

Garrison, D. R., Anderson, T., & Archer, W. (2000).Critical inquiry in a text-based environment: Computer conferencing in higher education. *The Internet and Higher Education, 2*(2-3), 1–19

Gutwin, C., & Greenberg, S. (2004). The importance of awareness for team cognition in distributed collaboration. In E. Salas & S.M. Fiore (Eds.), *Team cognition: Understanding the factors that drive process and performance* (pp. 177–201). Washington, DC: American Psychological Association.

Haake, J. M., & Pfister, H. R. (2007). Flexible scripting in net-based learning groups. In F. Fischer, I. Kollar, H. Mandl, & J. M. Haake (Eds.), *Scripting computer-supported collaborative learning: cognitive, computational and educational perspectives* (pp. 155–176). New York, NY: Springer.

Hall, E., & Hall, M. (1990). *Understanding cultural differences*. New York, NY: Intercultural Press.

Hmelo-Silver, C.E. (2004). Problem-based learning: What and how do students learn? *Educational Psychology Review, 16*(3), 235–266.

Janssen, J., Erkens, G., & Kanselaar, G. (2007). Visualization of agreement and discussion processes during computer-supported collaborative learning. *Computers in Human Behavior, 23*(3), 1105–1125.

Janssen, J., Erkens, G., Kanselaar, G., & Jaspers, J. (2006). Visualization of participation: Does it contribute to successful computer-supported collaborative learning? *Computers & Education, 49*(4), 1037–1065.

Janssen, J., Kirschner, F., Erkens, G., Kirschner, P. A., & Paas, F. (2010). Making the black box of collaborative learning transparent: combining process-oriented and cognitive load approaches. *Educational psychology review, 22,* 139–154.

Johnson, D. W., & Johnson, R. T. (1999). *Learning together and alone: cooperative, competitive, and individualistic learning* (5th ed.). Boston: Allyn & Bacon.

Jonassen, D. H. (1997). Instructional design models for well-structured and ill-structured problem-solving learning outcomes. *Educational Technology Research and Development, 45*(1), 65–94.

Jonassen, D. H. (2003). Using cognitive tools to represent problems. *Journal of Research on Technology in Education, 35*(3), 362–381.

Jung, H. (2010). *The effects of the types of collaboration script on collaboration load, collaboration process and outcome.* Unpublished doctoral dissertation, Hanyang University, Seoul, Korea.

Kim, S. (2009). *Design-based research of argumentation supporting tool in Wiki based computer-supported collaboration learning.* Unpublished doctoral dissertation, Hanyang University, Seoul, Korea.

Kimball, L. (1995). Ten ways to make online learning groups work. *Educational Leadership, 53*(2), 54–56.

King, A. (2007). Scripting collaborative learning processes: a cognitive perspective. In F. Fischer, I. Kollar, H. Mandl, & J. M. Haake (Eds.), *Scripting computer-supported collaborative learning: cognitive, computational and educational perspectives* (pp. 13–37). New York, NY: Springer.

Kirschner, P., Beers, P. J., Boshuizen, H. P. A., & Gijselaers, W. H. (2008). Coercing shared knowledge in collaborative learning environments. *Computers in Human Behavior, 24,* 403–420.

Kirschner, P., Strijbos, J. W., Kreijns, K., & Beers, P. J. (2004). Designing electronic collaborative learning environments. *Educational Technology Research and Development, 52*(3), 47–66.

Ko, G. (2010). *The effects of information types provided by activity awareness supporting tool on collaboration learning in CSCL environment.* Unpublished master's dissertation, Hanyang University, Seoul, Korea.

Kobbe, L., Weinberger, A., Dillenbourg, P., Harrer, A., Hamalanien, R., Hakkinen, P., & Fischer, F. (2007). Specifying computer-supported collaboration scripts. *Computer-Supported Collaborative Learning 2,* 211–224.

Kreijns, K., & Kirschner, P., A. (2004). Designing sociable CSCL environments. In J. Strijbos, P. A. Kirschner, & R. L. Martens (Eds.), *What we know about CSCL and implementing it in higher education* (pp. 221–243). Dordrecht, The Netherlands: Kluwer Academic Publishers.

Kuhn, D., Shaw, V., & Felton, M. (1997). Effects of dyadic interaction on argumentative reasoning. *Cognition and Instruction, 15,* 287–315.

Lave, J., & Wenger, E. (1991). *Situated learning: Legitimate peripheral participation.* Cambridge: Cambridge University Press.

Lipponen, L., Hakkarainen, K., & Paavola, S. (2004). Practices and orientations of CSCL. In J. Strijbos, P. A. Kirschner, & R. L. Martens (Eds.), *What we know about CSCL and implementing it in higher education* (pp. 31–50). Dordrecht, The Netherlands: Kluwer Academic Publishers.

Morse, K. (2003). Does one size fit all? Exploring asynchronous learning in a multicultural environment. *Journal of Asynchronous Learning Networks, 7*(1), 37–55.

Paavola, S., Lipponen, L., & Hakkarainen, K. (2004). Models of innovative knowledge communities and three metaphor of learning. *Review of Educational Research, 74*(4), 557–576.

Roschelle, J., & Teasley, S. (1995). The construction of shared knowledge in collaborative problem solving. In C. O'Malley (Ed.), *Computer-supported collaborative learning* (pp. 69–197). Berlin, Germany: Springer.

Rourke, L., Anderson, T., Garrison, D., R., & Archer, W. (1999). Assessing social presence in asynchronous text-based computer. *Journal of distance education, 14*(2), 50–71.

Rummel, N., & Spada, H. (2007). Can people learn computer-mediated collaboration by following a script? In F. Fischer, I. Kollar, H. Mandl, & J. M. Haake (Eds.), *Scripting computer-supported collaborative learning: cognitive, computational and educational perspectives* (pp. 39–55). New York, NY: Springer.

Scardamalia, M., & Bereiter, C. (1996). Computer support for knowledge-building communities. In T. Koschmann (Ed.), *CSCL: Theory and practice of an emerging paradigm* (pp. 249–265). Mahwah, NJ: Erlbaum.

Sfard, A. (1998). On two metaphors for learning and the danger of choosing just one. *Educational Researcher, 27,* 4–13.

Si, J. (2005). *Cultural comparison of students' role adjustment in online learning environments.* Unpublished master's dissertation, University of Toronto, Canada.

Stahl, G. (2004). Groupware goes to school: adapting BSCW to the classroom. *International Journal of computer applications in technology, 19*(3/4), 162–174.

Stahl, G., Koschmann, T., & Suthers, D. D. (2006). Computer-supported collaboration learning. In R.K. Sawyer (Ed.), *The Cambridge handbook of the learning sciences* (pp. 409–426). New York , NY: Cambridge University Press.

Stegmann, K., Weinberger, A., & Fischer, F. (2007). Facilitating argumentative knowledge construction with computer-supported collaboration scripts. *International Journal of computer-supported collaborative learning, 2*(4), 421–447.

Sun, J. (2010). *The design-based research of grounding supporting tools in wiki based computer-supported collaborative learning.* Unpublished doctoral dissertation, Hanyang University, Seoul, Korea.

Suthers, D. D. (2001). Towards a systematic study of representational guidance for collaborative learning discourse. *Journal of Universal Computer Science, 7*(3), 254–277.

Suthers, D. D. (2007). Roles of computational scripts. In F. Fischer, I. Kollar, H. Mandl, & J. M. Haake (Eds.), *Scripting computer-supported collaborative learning: cognitive, computational and educational perspectives* (pp. 177–187). New York, NY: Springer.

Suthers, D. D., Vatrapu, R., Medina, R., Joseph, S., & Dwyer, N. (2008). Beyond threaded discussion: representational guidance in asynchronous collaborative learning environments. *Computers & Education 50,* 1103–1127.

Sweller, J. (1998). Cognitive load during problem solving: effects on learning. *Cognitive Science, 12,* 257–285.

Sweller, J., & Chandler, P. (1994). Why some material is difficult to learn. *Cognition and Instruction, 12,* 185–233.

Weinberger, A. (2008). *CSCL Scripts: effects of social and epistemic scripts in computer-supported collaborative learning.* Saarbrücken, Germany: VDM Verlag.

Weinberger, A., Stegmann, K., Fischer, F., & Mandl, H. (2007). Scripting argumentative knowledge construction in computer-supported learning environments. In F. Fischer, I. Kollar, H. Mandl, & J. M. Haake (Eds.), *Scripting computer-supported collaborative learning: Cognitive, computational and educational perspectives* (pp. 191–212). New York, NY: Springer.

ABOUT THE AUTHORS

Lisa Bardwell is CEO of Earth Force, Inc. and earned her Ph.D. at the University of Michigan. Prior to joining Earth Force to help found the Denver office in 1997, Lisa taught at the University of Michigan, and in Utah and Colorado. She has always been committed to finding ways to better engage students in learning and their communities. Her expertise in community development, service-learning, environmental problem-solving, and how our environment influences people's well-being and ability to function made Earth Force a natural fit.

Tom Caswell is Open Education Policy Associate at the Washington State Board for Community and Technical Colleges (SBCTC). Tom earned his EdS degree in Instructional Technology and Learning Sciences from Utah State University. His current focus is expanding access to higher education through open education projects and policy work.

Chalee Engelhard is an Assistant Professor of Clinical at the University of Cincinnati. She serves as the Director of Clinical Education for the Physical Therapy Program. She earned her MBA from Thomas More College and is currently working towards her EdD in Instructional Design and Technology from the University of Cincinnati. Her research interests center on distance learning utilizing social media as well as implementing transformative modes of learning for clinical education.

Designing Problem-Driven Instruction with Online Social Media, pages 169–172
Copyright © 2012 by Information Age Publishing
169

Amy Frey Gerney is an Assistant Professor of Occupational Therapy at Ithaca College in Ithaca, New York. She received her doctoral degree in Occupational Therapy at Thomas Jefferson University and a Certificate in Distance Education from the University of Wisconsin-Madison. She has experience teaching competency based courses as well as with course design and development in blended learning environments at both the masters and doctoral levels. Her interests include the use of technology to facilitate formative student learning experiences.

Liz Henry is Director of Community Partnership for Earth Force, Inc. and leads several projects. Part of her responsibilities include maintaining Earth Force's social media presence. Liz earned a Master's Degree in Curriculum and Instruction, with a focus on Urban/Multicultural Education, from the University of Denver. Having implemented the CAPS process with her students, Liz now supports teachers bringing service learning into the classroom.

Marion Jensen is the founder of TwHistory.org and a PhD student at Utah State University in the Department of Instructional Technology and Learning Sciences.

Dongsik Kim is a Professor of the Department of Educational Technology at the Hanyang University in Seoul. Kim earned his Ph.D. in Instructional Systems & Technology from Florida State University in 1990. His research interests revolve around devising effective design principles of CSCL learning environments, developing instructional design components for maximizing learners' cognitive processing in e-learning for formal education and job-performance training sectors.

Seung H. Kim is currently an Associate Professor of College of Education and Program Director of Instructional Technology Master's program at Lewis University. She earned her EdD in Instructional Technology at the University of Houston. She has expertise in the areas of technology integration into curriculum, instructional design, web/multimedia development, interactive graphics, online learning, and teacher education. Her current research includes studies on the effect of students' usage of technology on their social/emotional network and investigating teachers' use of emerging Web 2.0 technology in instruction.

Victor R. Lee is an Assistant Professor in the Department of Instructional Technology and Learning Sciences at Utah State University. His work focuses largely on the design and study of technology-supported K–12 curriculum, instruction, and learning. His current work involves devising ways to use physical activity data devices as tools for student learning.

Cara Lynch is Director of Community Partnerships for Earth Force, Inc. She is a former high school English teacher, and is passionate about engaging students in authentic learning, poetry, and hiking. She supports schools, teachers, and community partners as they implement the Earth Force process into student learning opportunities.

Mary P. Mahaffey is a first-grade teacher at Harrisburg Academy. Mahaffey earned her MEd in Reading from Bloomsburg University. She serves as the lower school division chair where Mrs. Mahaffey advocates for online social media in the primary grades.

Marlene Joy Morgan is currently an Assistant Professor in the Department of Occupational Therapy at The University of Scranton in Scranton, Pennsylvania. Morgan received her doctorate in Educational Leadership and Policy studies from Temple University. Her areas of expertise are educational administration and curriculum development. Dr. Morgan's clinical focus is in the areas of gerontology and community based services. She has developed and engaged in on line education for both masters' and doctoral level occupational therapists.

Debra A. Pellegrino is a Professor of Education and Dean of the Professional College at the University of Scranton. The Panuska College of Professional Studies houses undergraduate and graduate programs in education, nursing, counseling, health administration, exercise sciences, physical therapy and occupational therapy. Pellegrino earned her EdD in Educational Leadership from Saint Louis University. Her research interests revolve around literacy learning and community collaboration between higher education and the K–12 school. Her recent research project focuses on examining collaborative approaches toward interprofessional education and its impact on healthcare and education.

Jen Richter is a doctoral candidate in the American Studies Program at the University of New Mexico in Albuquerque. She is interested in the cultural and political intersections of environment, science and technology. Specifically, her research focuses on the history and environmental issues of the Nuclear West. She is also active in the local community, exploring issues of science and society with various teen groups at the New Mexico Museum of Natural History and Science, as well as with the Earth Force organization that focused on the interactions of teens and food security, sustainability, and community action in Belen, NM.

Kay Kyeong-Ju Seo is an Assistant Professor of Instructional Design and Technology at the University of Cincinnati. Seo earned her PhD in Instructional Technology from Utah State University. Her research interests revolve around social cognitive development in 3D immersive virtual worlds, constructivist approaches to online social media, and technology integration in K–12 and higher education.

Brett E. Shelton is an Associate Professor in the Department of Instructional Technology and Learning Sciences at Utah State University. His research interests are instructional games, simulations, and immersive learning environments.

Jihyun Si is a PhD student in the Department of Educational Technology at Hanyang University in Seoul, Korea. Her recent interest areas are CSCL, sequencing methods, CLT, WOE, and online social media in higher education contexts.

Dana Tindall is the Associate Director for Learning Environments at Xavier University in Cincinnati, Ohio. He works in the area of faculty development, particularly with the implementation of successful online pedagogical strategies. His research interests are in online learning and the use of audio recording of reflection combined with use of online social communication tools.

Andrew Walker is an Associate Professor in the Department of Instructional Technology and Learning Sciences at Utah State University. He does research in technology teacher professional development, problem-based learning, and meta-analysis.

Ying Xie is an Assistant Professor in the Graduate Department of Educational Leadership and Instructional Design at Idaho State University. She earned her PhD in Instructional Systems from the Pennsylvania State University. Her current research focuses on design-based research, the integration of emerging technologies and creation of cognitive tools to promote reflective thinking, higher-order learning, and knowledge construction.

CPSIA information can be obtained at www.ICGtesting.com
Printed in the USA
BVOW032025130212

282570BV00003B/79/P